The Veteran Mentor's Guide To Baseball Coaching

Diamond Publishing Company
Cleveland, Ohio

The Veteran Mentor's Guide to Baseball Coaching
By Fred Heinlen

Diamond Publishing Company
3201 Enterprise Parkway, Suite 450
Beachwood OH 44122
(216) 896-9477, 1-888-WORKHRD (1-888-967-5473)

Limited First Edition: 2002
Printed in the United States of America

Library of Congress Control Number: 2002103844

ISBN: 0-9648710-4-1

Marketing and Media Relations:
            Penhallurick & Associates, Inc.
            Cleveland, Ohio
Cover Design: Concialdi Design, Frankfort, Illinois
Text Preparation: Kimmi DiLullo
Text Editing: Cheryl Broadway

The Veteran Mentor's Guide To Baseball Coaching

By Fred Heinlen

CONTENTS

PUBLISHER'S INTRODUCTION

A year ago, I suggested to Fred Heinlen, my former high school baseball coach and long-time real life mentor, that he write a book on his baseball philosophy and coaching techniques that he had developed over a 58 year career. I thought it would be a simple, straight forward project: he writes it; we do a little editing; we print a few copies.

Happily, the initial concept became much more than just helping Fred publish his baseball coaching book. It has been an exhilarating labor of love. Not only has Fred created the desired manual, but he has helped many former players and coaches rekindle their cherished memories. I have come to realize, more than ever, what a special, unique person Fred Heinlen is, not just in my mind, but in those of countless others.

Edited excerpts from correspondence with Fred's friends, former players and opposing coaches form their own special section of this book. They give the reader a clear insight into the character, commitment, dedication, educational philosophy and professionalism of a once in a lifetime person and coaching legend.

The readers will derive a double treat. They will enjoy intuitive sketches of a great man and learn the solid baseball fundamentals that will improve their enjoyment, understanding and playing of baseball---the greatest game ever invented!

This book is a legacy for Fred Heinlen, his family, his friends and his former student athletes. Hopefully it will be an inspiration for young players, their parents and aspiring coaches for generations to come.

Ned Grossman

UNIVERSITY SCHOOL

Athletic Department

8 Oct

Ned...

Can you make anything of the enclosed?????

Holy Toledo...I look at the enclosed/ enclosed and I realize...

        didn't invent anything
        discover anything
        didn't become President

but...gut...sure did have fun...and I'd like to do everything
exactly as did all over again...

Most of all I watched so many just like you...play a good game,

so...no regrets ...and...and...isn't that nice!!!

Hey...Be Good To You!!!

                               Blessings a-plenty,

                               Veteran Mentor

*Best of all - I got to meet Ned
Grossman !!!*

UPPER SCHOOL · 2785 S.O.M. CENTER ROAD · HUNTING VALLEY, OHIO · 44022
(216) 831-2200 · FAX (216) 292-7811 · www.upper.us.edu   RECYCLED AND RECYCLABLE

3

To my wife, Lois. Her constant support has enabled me to pursue this gift of baseball interest I have been given.

Fred Heinlen
55 Years of Coaching
  3 years of service ball
  1 year at an orphanage
  2 years New York State High School
  30 years Shaker Heights High School
  19 years Freshman Coach at University School

Notable achievements...2 Ohio High School AAA Championships.

Biography

♦ Graduated from Shaw High School and played baseball, basketball and football.
♦ Springfield College played baseball and basketball.
♦ Service Air Corp as a Physical Training Officer, played 3 years of Post baseball and 3 years of Post basketball. 5 years of service time, left as a Captain.
♦ Family: Wife Lois, married 59 years. Children: Doug, Rodd and Jan. 5 grandchildren.
♦ At Shaker High, coached basketball for 34 years, Assistant Football Coach and Athletic Director for 25 years.
♦ At Shaker High, coached 727 games, won 466, lost 261, winning percentage 64%.
♦ At University School, was Assistant Football Coach, Assistant Basketball Coach and Freshman Baseball Coach.
♦ Clinic Instructor for the Cleveland Indians for 10 years, teaching youth league players and coaches.
♦ Currently giving the same free clinics to youth league players and coaches.

6

INTRODUCTION

For 55 years of secondary school baseball coaching, and during another eight years of youth baseball instruction for the Cleveland Indians and after subsequent baseball clinics for youth league coaches and players, I always wanted to write an instruction manual for youth league coaches and players. It was all talk until now.

Nothing happened until my good friend and former Shaker Heights High School varsity baseball player, Ned Grossman, said; "Stop talking about writing your manual. Just do it!" So, here it goes.

Coaching all those years, certainly one would have to learn SOMETHING about baseball coaching. These suggestions have been the cornerstone of my way of coaching the game of baseball. This approach led to just three losing seasons in my 35 years as Varsity Baseball Coach at Shaker High. Two of those years ended with us winning the "big school" State Championship. Along the way, games were won when we shouldn't have won; games were lost when we shouldn't have lost.

What you will read is all practical, the way one coach did it. Nothing theoretical. It worked for me. Your way may be better. Use the following suggestions as a reference point relative to what you are doing. If you read these words and conclude that the way you are teaching baseball is superior, then this manual is a success!!!

Fred Heinlen

1

THOUGHTS FOR PARENTS

As parents, we all want our children to have productive, interesting lives as they are growing up. The key is to expose them to outlets that we, as parents, find interesting. We turn to sports, or to music or to art, whatever. We expose out children to "things" hoping a kernel of interest will develop that will keep them active and involved. Sometimes the exposure takes. Other times, it doesn't.

Encouragement, and more encouragement, is primary. Your youngster must receive satisfaction from his exposure. There must be constant success during every phase of baseball development.

Provide equipment commensurate with the age of your child: light bats and hitting large rubber balls that, when missed, will not hurt the child. Getting banged up with a hard ball is a sure way of losing interest in baseball. Not much fun if a child rarely hits the ball or constantly misses a ball because it is being batted or thrown too fast and too hard.

The key word is patience!!! Step-by-step: fly balls learned to be received via a tennis ball hit by a racket; ground balls learned to field properly via balls thrown against a wall; batting learned by pitching underhand at a short distance.   Step-by-step, all the while voicing encouragement.

Parent, you suggest going out and tossing the ball around. And, by all means, when your child suggests it, drop everything and join him in the backyard. There will come a time (and it comes in a hurry!) when such activity won't happen, or the child will come home and say: "No interest."

It is up to the child to nurture that interest, and not up to the parent to force an interest. Along the way, interests change. There is so much for a youngster to explore. It is one interest now and another shortly after. It happens frequently in baseball when a child will simply say, "I've found other interests. I'd like to give up baseball." He is aware of his limitations and realizes that his playing baseball is no longer productive. This is a child's decision and there isn't a thing a parent can do about it. Parent, let it go. Put your disappointment behind you and become interested in your child's latest interest. Not easily done.   I know, having gone through the experience.

Be it baseball, tennis or whatever the sport, it is a nice thing to have that interest at least through high school. It's a great way to keep open the doors of communication between parents and a child. It isn't the end of the world if one day your ball player comes home and tells you he doesn't want to play the game anymore.

An early background of playing sports provides a lifelong opportunity to go to games together, talk about games. It provides an avenue of communication. So, even if the exposure doesn't last too long, much has been gained by that experience and your parental interest.

Now, think of sports as a vehicle that enables your child to enjoy growing up. There comes a time when other things in life must be examined. Enjoy the sports experience with your child...it won't last forever but the memories will.

2

WHY "THE GREATS" ARE "THE GREATS"

We are not born with equal talent. Some are brighter; some run faster; some are better coordinated, etc; But, each one of us has the ability to explore, develop and maximize the potential we are gifted with.

A fairy tale illustrates the point. There was a big race between a hare and a turtle. Without question, the hare was thought to be a shoo-in winner. The race began. Immediately the hare ran off to a huge lead. He stopped to check on the turtle who was far, far behind. The hare took a nap while the turtle plodded on.

The hare woke in time to see the turtle drawing up beside him. Off went the hare to again establish a huge lead over the turtle. Again, the hare napped. The turtle just kept plodding away until he had caught up with the hare. The hare woke up and raced to another commanding lead.

The same thing happened again, but this time the hare failed to wake up in time. By the time he did, the turtle was far ahead and about to cross the finish line. The hare ran faster than ever to catch the turtle, but to no avail as the turtle crossed the finish line ahead of the hare to win the race.

♦　♦　♦　♦　♦

Three true stories come to mind which players should hear.

The first is about Babe Ruth. On a Sunday afternoon in 1930 at Philadelphia's Schibe Park (long since torn down), the Yankees and the A's were locked in a pennant chase. A capacity crowd came out to see "Lefty" Grove, having a Hall of Fame season, pitch to the Babe and his Yankees. As for Ruth, the fans came out to see him strike out or hit a home run...he was spectacular either way. Ruth didn't strike out that often, despite his slugging prowess. He never struck out 100 times in a season, but did hit in the .340's over his 20 plus major league seasons. He was a premier slugger who, in between hitting home runs, was a bat-ball contact hitter.

In the first inning Grove struck out the Babe. Ruth simply dropped his bat and slowly jogged back to his dugout. Next time at bat, Grove K'd Ruth again and the same thing happened. Ruth dropped the bat and slowly jogged back to the dugout. The next time at bat, the same thing happened. (It was easy to strike out against Grove.) Only this time, the Babe fell down with his huge frame covering every inch of home plate. The fans went wild....straw hats littered the field, scorecards came flying out of the stands amid cheering that went on and on. The Babe got up, dusted himself off and repeated his slow jog back to the dugout. The game was held up while the field was cleared of debris.

You know what's coming. Babe's final time at bat, score tied at 0-0. The first Grove pitch and WHACK, the Babe took the ball out of the park for a home run that

14

stood up for a Yankee 1-0 win. His return to the dugout was the same as when he struck out, no high fives, no waving of the cap, no arms in the air, just his slow trot to the dugout.

After the game, the Yankees sportswriters questioned Ruth about his lack of exuberance following his homer. They asked "Weren't you excited--- weren't you elated?" Ruth's reply was: "No need to get excited because the pitcher knew what I knew. Every time I struck out, I was that much closer to hitting my next home run and that's what I did."

The lesson for young players is....if you fail to make ball-bat contact, you are just that much closer to making contact. Failure is not taking the opportunity to go to bat again. There is always the opportunity to hit the ball if you forget your past failure and do battle with the pitcher again. The only failure is giving up.

◆ ◆ ◆ ◆ ◆

The second true story is how Joe DiMaggio played the game. A little over 3,000 fans were in the Comisky Park stands on a cold, drizzly fall night. The Yankees had already clinched the pennant. It was the last of the ninth inning with the Yankees comfortably ahead. With two outs, a Chicago batter hit a long fly ball to right centerfield. DiMaggio took off and, just in front of the wall, he leaped, caught the ball, crashed into the wall and down he went. He got up and jogged into the clubhouse.

Reporters surrounded him, each with the same question for Joe. Why had he taken the chance of injury in fielding the fly ball? The game for Chicago was out of reach. The pennant for the Yankees was already won. Why the effort to make a dangerous play? DiMaggio's reply was: "There might have been one fan in the stands who had never seen me play before." No wonder he is a Hall of Famer!!! DiMaggio's attitude has application to all your players. Go all out on every play. Let our play indicate to all the kind of player one is. A player's signature as to who I am as a ballplayer is to strive to give my best effort on EVERY play.

♦　♦　♦　♦　♦

This third true story also involves a Hall of Famer, Stan Musial, a life long .340 plus hitter for the St. Louis Cardinals, a premier hitter in the National League!!!

In his 24th season, he announced his retirement following the completion of the season. At the time of his announcement, he was hitting in the .340's. The media asked him why he was taking this step. Musial's replied that two weeks previously he had heard the hot dog vendors selling hotdogs. He realized he had lost his concentration while at bat. It was time, in his mind, to retire.

♦　♦　♦　♦　♦

Ruth, DiMaggio and Musial, all brought baseball "something special" to their play, something beyond their considerable Hall of Fame abilities. That "something special" was an ATTITUDE that demanded of them the total pursuit of realizing their full potential.

16

Now, few of us are going to become Hall of Famers. But these three players brought to the game an attitude that is possible for any player to adopt. Physically, most just can't cut it, but mentally all is within reach!!!

◆ ◆ ◆ ◆ ◆

And so it is with players and their physical baseball skills. Often the highly talented believe they don't have to work at developing those skills. The less talented player avails himself of every opportunity to practice, enabling him to develop his limited skills to the fullest potential. Players: DO AS THE TURTLE and you will be able to overcome the more gifted advantaged player! Pursue your dream to become a good ball player with never ending enthusiasm and a work ethic that will not be denied.

However, if the highly physically gifted player develops a work ethic that allows him to also develop his physical skills and to challenge his potential, he will win the race. But, the "turtle" ball player will have the satisfaction of having done his best. A worthy goal--- pursue it!!! Just never give up your pursuit to become a good ballplayer!!!

Players: no matter your interest, achievement can be yours ONLY through dedicated effort, working at the skills, practicing the skills. Unrelenting practice. Wishing will not do it. Hoping will not do it. Reading baseball magazines will not do it. ONLY practicing baseball skills will do it. Achievement can only be yours through constant effort!!! This is a fact!!!

3

NOMENCLATURE

Before we explore teaching the fundamentals, let us define the nomenclature. Coach: you know what you mean when instructing, but does your player? Do not back away from changing your instructional words. Change, if necessary, will contribute to your players understanding of what it is that you are trying to teach.

♦ ♦ ♦ ♦ ♦

As illustrated by the TV hit program, *Who wants to be a Millionaire*, we are all dumb about different things. As coaches, we know what we want a player to do, but does he know? It is our responsibility to explain the fundamentals in terms of their understanding. Different nomenclature and different approaches to teaching a skill are necessary for our players to grasp what we are attempting to teach. Say it in different ways because we are all dumb about different things.

♦ ♦ ♦ ♦ ♦

For instance, in place of the over used word "hustle," substitute the words, "AS IF;" "AS IF" the next pitched ball will be hit to you. Expecting the ball to come to them will put your fielders in a ready and alert position. You now have what you desire on defense relative to "hustle." A defensive team of alert players is in position to get a "jump" on the ball following every pitch.

A player who has not had a ball hit to him inning after inning soon grows complacent, becomes dead on his feet and finds his mind wandering. The coach calls out "hustle" to his team and the player simply does not do what you want him to do because nothing is happening to him. Call out "AS IF" and your players alert themselves to the possibility of the ball coming their way. Just those two words will make all the difference to your team in terms of "hustle."

Using the word "hustle" on a weak tap back to the pitcher is not going to help your runner. He questions your nomenclature because there is no way he is going to be safe. So why the word hustle? How many times have you seen a player give up on full-out effort to beat out a hit ball. He takes the attitude that he is going to be out. He assumes (broken down, the word assume can mean making an "ass" out of "u" and "me.") This player is playing the game "AS IF" the worst is going to happen to him, instead of adopting the attitude that the best is going to happen to him. By running all out, an ordinary ground ball can get the runner safely to first because the fielder must hurry the throw. The first baseman could take his foot off the base too soon. Run every hit ball "AS IF" the runner is going to be safe.

◆　◆　◆　◆　◆

The same words "AS IF" also have great significance to a batter. If he thinks the next pitch is his to hit "AS IF" the next pitch is THE one, the hitter will be so much better prepared to do just that. A change in attitude to, "this is my pitch to hit," will give you, the coach, ready hitters. The element of surprise will be eliminated because your batter will be ready for any pitch.

Playing the game "AS IF" the best thing is going to happen to a player results in the player's total concentration. Your players will be playing as you want them to play, when you used to call out "hustle." The word hustle now takes on a new and understandable meaning to your team. Try it!!!

♦ ♦ ♦ ♦ ♦

Words and phrases to eliminate:

- ♦ Get two. Replace with: "get one twice."
- ♦ Calling out to the pitcher: "Throw strikes!" He needs help to do just that. He does not need to be reminded that he is not throwing strikes.
- ♦ "You have to want it." Your players want to do well. Do not claim after a loss, "my kids didn't want it enough." A loss develops for many reasons, not because they "didn't want it enough." A player is bewildered by the statement. He does not have a clue as to what he is accused of. I have never known a player that did not want to field a ball cleanly or make the proper good throw or who didn't want to hit the ball. A silly, no-meaning statement that is not fair to your players. GET RID OF THE PHRASE!!!

♦ ♦ ♦ ♦ ♦

When calling off players in the pursuit of a fly ball, players should use the word "mine." It has a sharp sound to it and is easily understood. Once a player calls the word, other players get away. The player saying "mine" is responsible for pursuing the reception.

♦ ♦ ♦ ♦ ♦

I believe in locker room motivational signs. Your choices are as good as any. My favorites:

♦ "Count your blessings."
♦ "Proclaim your rarity."
♦ "Go the extra mile."
♦ "Use wisely your power of choice."

♦ ♦ ♦ ♦ ♦

My idea of the ultimate obscenity is the word "when." People say: "I will be OK *when*. I will play hard *when*." Don't say, "*When*." Instead say: I'm getting better no matter what. "When" is an excuse that must not be accepted!!!

4

BASIC PRACTICE PHILOSOPHY
AND SUGGESTIONS

Practice doesn't make perfect. Perfect practice does.

♦ ♦ ♦ ♦ ♦

Pay attention to details!!! Lose you must, but never because you were outworked!

♦ ♦ ♦ ♦ ♦

A written agenda for practice is a must. Otherwise, all too often, a practice will be "winged," resulting in playing a practice game and that is where boredom sets in. Plan and have it on paper!!!

♦ ♦ ♦ ♦ ♦

Before practice, assemble your players and explain the practice agenda. Have a beginning and an end to your practice sessions. At the end of practice, assemble again and review the practice.

♦ ♦ ♦ ♦ ♦

Make certain you have an agenda for game day. Schedule time for all that needs to be done. Make time for a "time" agenda.

♦ ♦ ♦ ♦ ♦

Not perfect practice, but practice perfectly. That should be your goal, coach. There is a right way to execute every facet of baseball play. See to it that everything you do is directed towards pursuing the goal of skill perfection. Repetition of a skill, over and over, done perfectly is the key.

♦ ♦ ♦ ♦ ♦

Your main focus is to prepare your team to play solid fundamental baseball, enabling your team to compete evenly with your opponents, thus giving the opportunity to win games.

♦ ♦ ♦ ♦ ♦

Coach, you are playing the game with kids. Do not expect robot play from them, where a mistake is never made or where every ball hit is a hit. Playing the game with robots would be totally boring!!!

♦ ♦ ♦ ♦ ♦

Obviously there are many team fundamentals to cover. Do not try to cover everything in one practice. You have the entire season to cover all the basics and situations. Choose only one or two team play fundamentals per practice and work on them in-depth.

Team fundamentals include lead-offs and steals; catchers throwing to bases on steals; double-plays with runners running; covering bunts; the squeeze bunt, both safe and suicide---both from defensive and offensive standpoints. Take nothing for granted. What you don't cover will cost you a game sometime during the season.

♦ ♦ ♦ ♦ ♦

Do not abandon practice time for playing games. The recommended ratio is two practices to every game. Playing many games in lieu of practices is simply a lazy way to coach.

♦ ♦ ♦ ♦ ♦

Players must practice and play the game with the thought that: "This is who I am, not what I say I am. By my actions, I demonstrate who I am." After each baseball session, a player should be proud of himself through his effort.

With each practice, your aim is for your players to reach more fully their potential, to become the best they can be. A player does not achieve his baseball potential in one practice. A building goes up one brick at a time. So it is with developing into a "good" ballplayer. One practice at a time, with each practice contributing to his goal of improving as a ballplayer. Patience. Developing proper baseball skills is a slow process. There is no room for discouragement!!!

Coaches: have patience. One building block at a time. One baseball skill at a time and soon you will have covered, in practice, a multiple number of the needed baseball skills that will enable your team to play sound baseball, competitive baseball.

♦ ♦ ♦ ♦ ♦

I once saw a sign in an elementary school classroom on the wall behind the teacher's desk. It read:

I hear and I forget.
I see and I remember.
I do and I understand.

♦ ♦ ♦ ♦ ♦

It is paramount for coaches to learn: don't talk so much. By talking too much you risk losing your players to boredom. There is a better way to learn. Demonstrate the skill you wish to teach your players and they will have an understanding of the skill to be learned. Then, have them practice that skill. Through visualization and continued practice, they will learn and succeed in accomplishing a baseball skill that is being taught.

A quote by George Allen (former NFL coach and a Super Bowl winner) says it all: "Winning can be defined as the science of being totally prepared." With that attitude, plus YOUR OWN INNOVATIVE APPROACH TO COACHING BASEBALL, you certainly have enough resources to cover the basics of sound baseball coaching. You have no reason for conducting boring practices---practices in which your team fails to improve with each practice, both on an individual basis and on a team basis.

♦ ♦ ♦ ♦ ♦

A basic tenet to coaching/teaching baseball is....TEACH, DON'T YELL!!! All players want to do the right thing on the field. It is our job, as coaches, to make certain they know what they are doing.

♦　♦　♦　♦　♦

Tim Gallway, the renowned author of *The Inner Game of Tennis*, learned a valuable lesson during a two week period when he had lost his voice. During those two weeks, he was reduced to <u>demonstrating</u> tennis strokes vs. <u>talking about</u> tennis strokes. His students learned by watching and then mimicking what they had watched. Much to his amazement, his students progressed much more rapidly than at any previous time.

This same concept is best illustrated by a child accomplishing the most difficult physical skill he will develop. The child learned to walk!!! No one taught him that skill. It was learned by watching, then mimicking what was observed. Once ready, and having observed those around him walking, the child stood, and with wobbly steps and after repeated failures to maintain his balance, finally took off.

And here an important baseball lesson can be learned. The child, no matter the repeated failed attempts to walk, always attempted it again, demonstrating the Japanese Proverb: "Fall down seven times, get up eight." This approach has significance to all baseball skills. Failure is not striking out seven times. Failure is not getting up to hit the eighth time!

♦　♦　♦　♦　♦

Try hard not to pre-judge a player. Hairstyle, for instance, does not matter. Salute the best in every kid playing for you. Be aware that each player is an individual unlike another. Pay homage to that individuality. Remember coach, we cannot all be like you and think like you. Respect the differences.

♦　♦　♦　♦　♦

Touch or speak to each player on your squad at every practice or game. Do not ignore the least of your players because your interest is only with your "star" players. The end of the bench player has a need to feel important to the team. With your effort, you will create a positive morale factor on your team.

♦　♦　♦　♦　♦

Coaches, always wear something that indicates to your players that the practice or the game means something to you. Show up wearing a T-shirt or a sweatshirt, at least a baseball cap. Such a simple thing will send a message to your players that you attach importance to that practice or game.

♦　♦　♦　♦　♦

Do not use exercise as a form of punishment. Exercise must be thought of as a privilege, not something to avoid. Instead of push-ups or laps, drill a player in the fundamentals he violated!!!

A player cannot always help it if he is late for practice or a game. Just demand a note from a teacher or parent and accept that note. No note, no practice or game.

◆　◆　◆　◆　◆

You, as a coach, must be selective in your praise. Players must not expect praise every time they execute a skill satisfactorily. It does not take long for a player to expect praise. Offer too much praise and the praise loses its meaning. No matter what, save praise for special moments.

The same happens when constant critical comments are made to players. Work on why a ground ball was missed and eliminate yelling negative things to the player. Remember, the player involved wanted to execute in a positive manner more than anyone on his team.

◆　◆　◆　◆　◆

Hit tennis balls with a tennis racquet to players at each infield position. Outfielders join the infielders. No throws involved. Just practice fielding ground balls to make certain your players are watching the ball go into their gloves. Next, bobbing the head into the glove, have them remove their glove and field the tennis balls bare handed. Tennis racquets and tennis balls also afford an excellent opportunity to work on pop ups.

◆　◆　◆　◆　◆

To renew your players enthusiasm for practice, do not hesitate to give players a day off. Give your players time removed from you and from baseball. Give them time to do things unrelated to baseball. A day off might provide the best kind of practice you could have.

♦　♦　♦　♦　♦

As part of your batting program make room for that old stand by, the pepper drill....one batter, three fielders. 15 feet separate the fielders from the batter. Choked up bat, half swing, promotes the head on the ball at ball-bat contact.

♦　♦　♦　♦　♦

Instead of the usual "situation" drill, play a game you have all played, called move-up. Put a team on the field with the rest of your squad hitting. No catcher, no strike-outs, no stealing, no walks....batter makes an out, he goes to right field and all others move to the next defensive position. Batter does not make an out, he stays batting. He can not be forced out if he is base runner. This "situation" gives all your players the opportunity to play different positions.

♦　♦　♦　♦　♦

A fun exercise your players will enjoy is to have a phantom infield drill. Have a regular infield without the ball. It's an enjoyable drill that makes for something different than the ordinary.

Players and parents must understand that playing at the varsity level is no longer based on rules mandating that all players on the squad play at least three innings of every game. At the high school level, you are playing games to win, resulting in your best players dominating playing time. Varsity sports is the equivalent of the higher level academic programs. Not all players qualify for the "honors courses."

◆　◆　◆　◆　◆

You want to earn your player's respect rather than gearing your coaching efforts to being "liked" or being a "buddy."

◆　◆　◆　◆　◆

Coaching is not a popularity contest. Some players might "like" you. The reverse may be true. You can not coach with the thought that you want players to "like" you. Certainly, you do not want your players to "dislike" you. It just shouldn't be a high priority with you. This philosophy holds true for the parents also. Parents of the players who play will be just fine. Expect parents of the players not playing to be critical of your coaching. That is just the way it is!

◆　◆　◆　◆　◆

Coaches must be aware that parents view their player subjectively, not objectively. Only you, coach, will see a player objectively. Many times a minor conflict occurs because of the different ways a player is viewed. A player might be on the bench only because other players on the team are better players. You, coach, must accept this responsibility, whereas a parent has great difficulty accepting the situation. Expect conflicts in this area. It comes with the territory.

You must realize that parents are primarily concerned with the play of their child and secondarily they are concerned with the winning or losing of a game. You simply have to appreciate where a parent is coming from and deal with that situation on an even keel. Many times this is difficult to do but...it is a must do!!!

♦ ♦ ♦ ♦ ♦

Make certain that in your practice sessions equal time is given to the non-starting player. Your aim is to see that ALL of your players are given the opportunity to improve their play.

♦ ♦ ♦ ♦ ♦

This, above all, NEVER embarrass one of your players before his teammates or your fans. When being upset by an individual, indicate that displeasure privately. The player does not need to be embarrassed in front of the entire squad. There is time to point out mistakes at your next practice or with controlled talk during a game.

Hey, no one ever said coaching a group of baseball kids was easy.

♦ ♦ ♦ ♦ ♦

There will be times when you, as a coach, will have good reason to lose your cool, to be upset not because of mechanical errors, but from an attitude stand point. This is the time to "blast" your team. It could happen a couple of times in the season. If you are not satisfied with your team's approach to the game, let them know it in no uncertain terms. A wake up call is necessary every once in awhile!!!

♦ ♦ ♦ ♦ ♦

Along the way in my 58 years of baseball coaching/teaching, I used this exercise to illustrate the importance of practicing a skill. Before a player could get a uniform, he had to juggle three tennis balls. Tennis balls would be issued to each player on a Monday, with the test to follow the next Monday. Initial efforts were what one might expect: tennis balls falling all over the place. However, by the next Monday test, each player could juggle the three tennis balls, not as an advanced juggler would do, but the players did accomplish the skill.

This exercise demonstrated to the players the rewards of practicing. YOU WILL DO IF YOU DO!!! The baseball application is evident. The skills required to play the game can be developed only through constant practice!!! So, coaches and players, if you haven't practiced a team skill or an individual skill, do not expect success relative to that skill.

♦ ♦ ♦ ♦ ♦

Coach, trust yourself and the way you teach baseball. Your approach, your drills, your way of doing things could bring new insights to coaching baseball. Mimic others if you must, but do not hesitate to challenge accepted methods in favor of your own way of doing things.

Here is an illustration of how original thinking can help in coaching. I finished giving a clinic in North Ridgeville, Ohio. We had spent time on the importance of watching the ball when hitting. A retired lady librarian, who was a successful coach for a high school girls' softball team, offered her solution to this important fundamental of watching the ball during the entire execution of hitting mechanics. She had taken two dozen softballs and painted one side yellow and one side blue. During batting practice she would ask each girl, following her hitting attempt, to tell her which color she hit. What a unique approach!!! Original!!!

So, coach, follow this example and pursue your own way of doing things. Just trust yourself!!! Reject others by saying: hey, my way is better!!!

◆　◆　◆　◆　◆

Whittaker Chambers, in his book *Witness*, offers this insight to living: "We are gifted with 24 hours of time in a day, no more, no less....Really, the only equal thing we have with one another. Some are brighter, stronger, can run faster, taller, etc; But, we are equal in time allotted us in a day. At the end of each day, we should be able to look back on the 24 hours spent and ask ourselves, did we get value received for the great price we paid (24 hours of our time)? Such time spent, we will never be able to get it back. Was the price of time worthwhile?"

You and your players should be aware of this special gift, time. Ask yourselves, was the two hours spent with baseball worth the time? After a practice or a game, was the time I gave worthwhile? Do I have regrets? Were those baseball efforts worth my precious time?

Both players and coaches, should come off the practice field, or following a game, having NO REGRETS. On that day the feeling should be, I left myself on that field. I did my best. I am pleased with my two hours spent with baseball. There is no way of knowing whether a coach or a player will be given the gift of another practice or game. It is a kind of morbid thought, but a thought that demands awareness.   Make your last practice or game the best of your efforts!!!

5

SPECIFIC PRACTICE TECHNIQUES

Coaches: You have no more important segment related to your practice than proper warm up. Never, never say to your team, "warm up." The traditional way is to toss the ball between two players and then walk away without supervising the warm up. This warm up period is a time players get lax and sloppy. They receive the ball with one hand, throw the ball without a target in mind, drop the ball and pick it up with the glove hand. This back and forth toss is a time for executing all skills properly.

♦　♦　♦　♦　♦

In your practice sessions, make certain that your players are doing just that, practicing. From the thousands of kids who start out in youth leagues, we lose many players because of boredom!!! By the time youngsters get to high school, the high school coach scrambles to find enough decent players to field a competitive team. See to it that your players aren't standing around doing nothing. How?

♦ Avoid hitting ground balls to just one player. Have your players roll ground balls to each other. You not only keep your players active, but this drill affords you the opportunity to correct players' technical flaws. The emphasis is to field the ball cleanly with

perfect technique. Every rolled ground ball should
be fielded with perfect form.

♦ For the outfielders, avoid hitting one ball to one
   player while eight or nine stand around.   Use a
   tennis racquet and tennis balls to hit to groups of no
   more than three players. Players can hit to each
   other.   Your aim is lots of repetitions, all done
   perfectly.

♦   ♦   ♦   ♦   ♦

Pop flies may be practiced the same way as fielding
ground balls. The proper technique is....get under the
ball so that if the pop up is missed, the ball would hit the
player on the forehead. On pop ups, locate the ball, get
under it, then receive it. Avoid, if possible, receiving the
ball on the run.

INFIELD PRACTICE ROUTINE

Hit or throw ground balls to your third baseman who
then throws to first; the target being the face of the first
basemen. The first baseman must not receive the throw
with his foot on top of the base. His foot should be
placed along the infield edge of the base. The entire foot
must make contact with the base.

While this practice is going on, hit or throw ground balls
to the shortstop and second baseman. They, in turn,
make the throw to the second base bag with the shortstop
and second baseman alternatingly receiving the ball.
Receive the throw with the left foot on the base. Then in
preparation for the throw to the first baseman the double

play attempt mechanic is a "crow hop" to the left or right of the bag for the shortstop, and a "crow hop" across the bag or back from the bag by the second baseman.

Then the third baseman throws to the second baseman while the shortstop makes his ground ball reception and throws to the first baseman. The second baseman fields his ground ball and makes his throw to third. After 20-25 such fielding plays, have the second baseman throw his ground ball reception to first base, while the shortstop makes his throw to third. The third baseman fields his ground ball and tosses the ball back to the hitter, or thrower, of the ground ball.

Time for the first baseman to do his base throwing to second and to third. Throws to second base must be made to the side of the runner. Throws must never come from a position directly behind a runner. His teammate must see the ball at all times!!! .

♦　♦　♦　♦　♦

Now practice the double play throws. The nomenclature is <u>not</u> "get two." It is "get one twice." Too often, a team hurries the play to the extent that no outs are recorded. Make certain of one out! Then, try for the second out. "GET ONE TWICE" slows things down enough that accurate throws have a better chance of being made.

Be satisfied with getting one out. Then the possibility is still there to get the second out. You must get one out before getting two!!!

♦　♦　♦　♦　♦

Meanwhile, your catchers are doing their "thing" off to one side, fielding bunts and throwing to first, footwork ("crow hop") on throws to second and third. When fielding bunts, the player should turn, facing the base he is to throw to, before the bunt is fielded. Teaching point: watch the ball go in to the throwing hand; be in position so your "crow hop" takes you toward the base the ball is being thrown to.

Catchers must practice foul pop ups. These fielding chances are not easy. The catcher takes his mask off, holds it until the ball is located, then discards his mask with a strong toss away from the direction of the catcher's run to the ball. Get under the ball, as another infielder would do. If missed, the ball would hit the catcher on the forehead.

◆ ◆ ◆ ◆ ◆

Meanwhile, outfielders are receiving balls and throwing to a cut-off man. Note: Have all three outfielders fielding balls at the same time with each throwing (obviously) to a different base. You now have all outfield positions drilling vs. one outfielder fielding with the other position outfielders standing around. Keeping everyone busy is the key to a good practice.

Cut-off players must receive the throw on their glove hand side, then follow the glove in a half turn to their target and throw with a "crow hop." The ball must be received with two hands so a throw can be made immediately upon reception.

♦ ♦ ♦ ♦ ♦

Coaches, let no mistake go uncorrected!!! If an infielder mishandles a ground ball, take the time to roll him a couple of balls so he ends that situation having been successful in handling a grounder. Whatever the mistake, dropped fly ball, poor throw or bad base running mistake, stop the practice and repeat the play until it is done successfully.

♦ ♦ ♦ ♦ ♦

At every practice, set aside a half hour to play the game. I call my game drill "situation," soft pitching, no catcher, no stealing. Obviously, no walks or strikeouts. But, otherwise, you simply play the game with the resulting situations of a regular game taking place.

Place your first team in the field and keep them there for 15-18 outs. The bases are cleared after every three outs. Pitchers do the soft toss pitching, enabling them to work on the demands of their position. Players not in the field are the offense. After the prescribed number of outs, switch players, enabling all of your players to gain real game "situation" experience. "Situation" is simply playing slow pitch hardball. It's a fun drill for your players and affords you, the coach, the opportunity to make sure that things are being done right.

Your players will enjoy this part of your practice so much because they are now playing the game of baseball versus just practicing various aspects of the game. Coaches, you will enjoy this segment of your practice because you may correct mistakes that occur both offensively and defensively.

◆　◆　◆　◆　◆

What you do cover in practice, cover in depth, in detail. What you do not cover in one practice, cover at your next practice. In your practices, there must be time to briefly review past team fundamentals. Not covering a situation could very well cost you a game. There must be a repetition of drills throughout the season. Keep a record of things covered!!!

6

PITCHING

The most important aspect of baseball, no matter what the level of play, little league through the majors, is found in the center of the infield...the PITCHER!!! Pitching is the essence of the game. If you have a couple of pitchers, you will win. No pitching, and no matter your coaching knowledge, your chances of winning are slim.

This, above all. If you find a player whose ball "moves" when he throws it, adopt him. Have him live with you. Do not let him out of your sight!!! These kinds of players are hard to find.

To find your pitchers, line up your players at shortstop and have them throw to first base. Strongest arms become your pitchers.

If a player without a strong arm does not throw the ball fast, he can still make a contribution to your team by becoming a curve ball pitcher. At 15, he is old enough to throw the curve ball. No matter the level of play, curve balls are not easy to hit. Throwing the curve ball for strikes will enable that player to win games for you.

Pitching, not throwing. There is a difference!!! It is a must for the pitcher to have a specific target. That target is the catcher's glove held high, positioned over the middle of the plate. Focus on the target begins with the wind-up and is never lost throughout the delivery of the ball. The target will be missed enough times so that corners of the plate will develop. Pitching to corners, at this level, leads to walks. Mental imaging comes in to play. The pitcher must imagine the ball going to the catcher's target.

A common fault is that the pitcher focuses on the batter. As a result, balls are consistently pitched away from the batter for called balls. Pitchers must see only their target and avoid seeing the batter.

Indoors in pre-season, draw the strike zone on the wall. It really is a big target. Seeing the large strike area is most helpful in establishing control. By seeing how big the strike zone target is, the pitcher will become confident in hitting that large area with his pitch.

Everything begins with the delivery, which can be perfected during your pre-season indoor pitching practice. Practice the delivery motion, step-by-step, so that your pitchers will deliver the perfect motion time after time. He must get to the point that the motion becomes automatic. Then the pitcher no longer has to think about his mechanics.

Your pitcher should not pitch with the thought that he does not want the batter to hit the ball. Walking batters takes the fun out of defense. The team loses interest, resulting in the defense being unprepared to get the jump on the ball to make needed defensive plays. After a delivery, the pitcher must realize that there are nine players ready to field the ball.

To pitchers, if you fall behind in the count, all it means is you must throw a strike ball on the next pitch. A 3-0 count does not mean a walk is automatic. Do not give in to the batter with a count in his favor. To pitchers, so many times you defeat yourself by thinking, "How can I pitch winning ball for seven innings?" Do not think in terms of seven innings. Think segments of the game, not the whole game. Think of pitching shutout ball for one inning, seven times. Reduce your thinking to one inning, one out, one batter at a time.

◆ ◆ ◆ ◆ ◆

Mechanically, the direction of the pitcher's stride is of major importance. Imagine a straight line from the pitching rubber to home plate. The pitcher's forward foot must land to the left of that imaginary line (right handed pitcher). This form enables the pitcher to deliver the ball with open hips. Along with the open stride (a must), the pitcher must land on the ball of his foot vs. pitching against a dug in heel. Landing on the front part of the foot permits the pitcher to get on top of his delivery.

◆ ◆ ◆ ◆ ◆

Holding the arm away from the body, with the ball held high, will permit the pitcher to throw the ball down. This downward, on top of the ball, motion greatly increases the delivery needed for consistent control. Following the release of the ball, the hand and wrist end up in a "fish hook" position.

A drill that promotes the throwing down on the ball motion is to station your pitchers 30 feet from a wall or fence. With the throw (pitch), bounce the ball 10 feet in front of the wall. This drill should imitate a pitcher's warm-up. Proper stride, open up, correct planting of the lead foot, arm away from the body with the ball held high---all mechanical aspects of pitching that must be watched closely.

A key point in the development of control is for the pitcher to keep continued arm movement after the ball is released. The arm doesn't stop until it no longer can extend itself. The pitcher should end up with the back of his shoulder facing the catcher. By doing this, the pitcher will have a viable follow through which is necessary for control.

♦　♦　♦　♦　♦

A word about the curve ball: it should be released at the batter's shoulder nearest the pitcher. It should be thrown so that if the ball does not curve it would hit the batter at the point of that shoulder. If a right handed pitcher is pitching to a left handed batter, he must imagine his release point as the same point as if he were pitching to a right handed batter. The reverse is true for a left handed pitcher. The pitcher should imagine the ball breaking over the plate. Never mind hitting the outside low corner. Just get it to break for a strike.

A quick breaking curve used to be called a hook. To accomplish a hook, the ball must be held tightly off the fast ball delivery. The speed of the pitch, plus a tight spin of the ball, will result in a quick breaking pitch.

46

With a slow curve ball, the release is the same, but the ball is held loosely, resulting in a slow ball rotation. Both the quick curve and the slow curve must have the identical pitching motion. Using the four seam grip on the ball, the spin for the curve ball comes from moving the middle finger to placement along the seam of the ball. The ball spin comes from pulling down on that seam with the middle finger grip.

When pitching the fast ball, a seam must be held by the two fingers that hold the ball with the thumb underneath. When the ball is released, the tips of those fingers must pull down severely in order to get reverse motion on the ball. The speed of the spin enhances the possibility of getting movement on the fast ball.

♦　♦　♦　♦　♦

At the high school level, use just three pitches: the fast ball, curve ball and change-up of both pitches. Work on being able to throw strikes with these three pitches. Trick pitches are simply not needed. There is time enough for trick pitches later on in a pitcher's development.

Perish the thought that, when ahead in the count, you can afford to waste pitches. Just keep getting the ball over the plate. Just keep throwing strikes and avoid getting "cute."

Most line-ups, short of advanced play, might have at the most three or four good hitters. Do your part by keeping runners off the bases via walks. Let your teammates make the routine plays, thereby avoiding big scoring innings by your opponents.

◆ ◆ ◆ ◆ ◆

Until you plant your foot on the pitching rubber, you are just another fielder. Once you place your foot on that rubber, you become a pitcher by position and are now subject to some specific rules. There is only one way to release yourself from the rubber and that is by stepping back from that rubber. Stepping forward with men on base results in a balk.

◆ ◆ ◆ ◆ ◆

When holding runners on base following your stretch, do not ignore them. Just make the runners stop their leading off strides. Before delivering a pitch, make sure you look at the runner. By stepping back off the rubber, you will force the runner to retreat to his base. Letting the runner know that you are attentive to him will prevent him from taking liberties in his lead-off. Look at him and then deliver.

As for attempting to pick-off runners, most often it is a waste of time. So many times the pick-off attempt results in a wild throw, with runners having no trouble advancing a base.

◆ ◆ ◆ ◆ ◆

A fundamental that cannot be ignored is taking the signal properly. You have to make sure you stay interested in all the signals given. Signals can be stolen if the first sign is the only signal you stay interested in. Ignoring signals, after the pitch is signaled, is a real give away to what pitch is coming.

◆　◆　◆　◆　◆

Another fundamental is pitchers fielding their position. Once the ball is pitched, a pitcher now becomes another infielder and must fulfill the responsibilities of his position.　The key for a pitcher throwing to bases following fielding a ball is to follow his glove to the base being thrown at.　Left handed player throwing to first,　follow the glove in a half turn, then throw.　Right handed players throwing to a base make the turn by following the glove.　By following the glove, the thrower gets a more fluid delivery of his throw.

◆　◆　◆　◆　◆

Covering bunts must be practiced by the pitcher.　With no one on base, the catcher, pitcher, third baseman and first baseman all charge, with the second baseman covering first.

◆　◆　◆　◆　◆

The pitcher is also responsible for covering first on double play attempts.　First baseman throws to the shortstop.　When the first baseman can not get back to first to complete the play, then the throw back to first has the pitcher covering.

Pitchers, you have back-up responsibilities that must be met. On throws from the outfield to third and to the plate, it is your responsibility to back-up.

On bunting responsibilities, pitchers are a key player. With a man on first, you must cover the area between the third baseman's charge and the charge of the first baseman. With a man on second, you must come off the rubber at an angle favoring third base. You and the first baseman are now charged with covering the same territory that three of you cover with just a man on first. With the man on second, the third baseman covers third base for the possible force play.

In defending the squeeze bunt, glance at the runner leading-off from third. If the squeeze is not detected, then right away the runner will take off for home before your delivery. You must see this and pitch high and tight to the batter, forcing him from the batter's box, giving your catcher a clear shot at blocking home plate and making the tag. If the squeeze is executed properly, it is a difficult play to defense. Just make certain you glance at the runner before your delivery.

♦ ♦ ♦ ♦ ♦

On throws from the outfield, the pitcher has the responsibility of backing up third and home, depending upon the play to be made. When outfielders are throwing to either of these bases, your pitcher must break from the mound and cover. Do not take such coverage for granted. If not practiced, such back-up duties just will not happen in a game.

♦ ♦ ♦ ♦ ♦

Pitchers, your response to errors and mistakes by your teammates is an important element to your success as a pitcher. Baseball is a simple game, but the most difficult of all games to play. Dismiss errors. They are going to happen!!! If you walk a batter, you do not expect body language of disgust from your fielders. By the same token, do not show body language disgust with fielding mistakes. Your teammates are not robots. Your fielders will not be helped by your negative reaction following an error. Dwelling on past plays will get you nowhere. You all need each other. So help one another via encouragement.

An important part of pitching involves your relationship with the umpire. Accept a call and go on from there. The umpires at the high school level and below are not professional umpires anymore than you are a professional pitcher. Once you get upset with ball and strike calls, you are in deep trouble. Your concentration and the job of pitching is lost. Go about your job. During the course of a game, umpire calls will even out.

7

BATTING

Sure You Can Hit The Ball!

As coaches, we all too often embrace the thought that hitting a ball can't be taught. Nonsense!!! Hitting home runs can't be taught (that kind of timing and power are gifts), but just plain ball-bat contact <u>can</u> be taught. Only by ball-bat contact will base hits result. You must first hit the ball before the base hits happen. We are simply talking about hitting the ball, not about batting averages. The main reason hitting is thought of as so difficult is because it is the least practiced of all the skills needed to play the game well.

◆　◆　◆　◆　◆

We will begin with the player's stance. Accept what the player feels comfortable with. Do not force a stance that a player feels is not for him. But, whatever the stance, there are some basics. The head must be turned so the batter can see the ball with both eyes vs. a "peek-a-boo" look, with one eye peeking over one shoulder. The hands and arms should be away from the body, in a boxer's hand and arm position.

Every pitcher has a release point for the ball delivery. Your hitter must focus on that vacant circle, from which the ball will eventually appear. By focusing upon that exact release point, the batter gets a maximum look at the ball for the full pitching distance. With practice, a batter will develop the needed concentration to zero in on that all important release point. The batter must school himself to ignore distractions, like dogs or kids running beyond the outfielders or comments from the stands (especially those comments directed at the umpires by grandmothers!). The attention on the ball release point must be total.

♦ ♦ ♦ ♦ ♦

Coaches: get rid of the term "swing!" Substitute the word EXPLODE!!! You demonstrate this mechanic by having players practice killing a fly. One does not swing at a fly. One explodes the swatter with a short stroke with as much speed as can be mustered. When swatting that fly, one looks at the fly until the swat is completed. So it is with hitting a ball. Total sight on the ball through the completion of the explosion. From nothing to EVERYTHING!

A major flaw in hitting (or not-hitting) is turning the head away from the ball at the time there should be contact. Batters find themselves looking out over foul territory when the head should be focused on the ball. Words that will help steady the head are: bite the ball during the explosion; and bury one's head over the plate when the explosion is finished. This mechanic can be developed through slow pitch batting practice. The ball is the "fly;" the bat is the "swatter." Each of your players knows exactly what you are demanding of them: explode and watch the target (ball).

♦ ♦ ♦ ♦ ♦

The use of visualization, mental imaging, is IMPORTANT. The batter must "see" the ball exploding and flying off the bat as a hard-hit line drive. By mental imagining, the body will adjust to a level explosion, enabling the batter to get the bat head out in front of the plate, rather than hitting the ball with the arms not extended.

♦ ♦ ♦ ♦ ♦

A great help in developing bat speed is lining up the small knuckles past the big knuckles. By holding the bat with one's hands in this position, it becomes automatic that the end of the bat speeds up upon ball impact.

♦ ♦ ♦ ♦ ♦

The fundamentals of lifting of the heel, the stride and the explosion can all be developed, enabling your player to learn these mechanics without thinking. The lifting of the heel upon delivery is a coiling mechanism, a "gathering" device much like a snake "gathers" before striking. The pitcher stands about 15 feet away from his batting partner. Then switch positions, the thrower to batter and batter to thrower. In a short time, each of your players will have accomplished a hundred explosions.

♦ ♦ ♦ ♦ ♦

Have your players attempt to "pull" every pitch. This thought generates bat speed and contributes to a pitched ball being hit HARD!!! Will every ball be pulled? No. But something will be done "right" by the batter vs. no visualization at all. Think: pull; line drive; ball hit hard and good things will happen. You very well might not agree with this thought, but it worked for me.

◆ ◆ ◆ ◆ ◆

Run your batting practice from three different spots simultaneously: off the fence on the first base side; from home plate; and from the fence on the third base side. With just one batting location, you will find yourself with a squad of players standing around. Have your players throw slowly, with no catcher and six players at each station: batter, foul ball chaser behind the batter, a thrower, a feeder, and two outfielders. Allow eight "nicks" and then players move up. Foul balls qualify as a "nick."

◆ ◆ ◆ ◆ ◆

For indoor and home hitting practice, give this a try: hit badminton birds, a sure method of developing good hitting habits. With badminton birds, your entire squad is busy.

◆ ◆ ◆ ◆ ◆

Coach: this practice is the time to check head position, quickness of bat, etc. Players use badminton birds in their backyards to go along with hitting a ball off a tee into a blanket set up in the garage or basement. Hitting can be practiced and practiced constantly. By constant practice, the batter will be able to focus completely on the pitched ball.

At one time, walking was the most difficult challenge a person had. But, through constant practice, it didn't take long to walk without giving the mechanics a thought. So it is with batting. Repetition and the hitting mechanics will be automatic. Then it is easy. See the ball and hit it!!!

♦   ♦   ♦   ♦   ♦

Encourage players at a young age to attempt to become switch hitters. The only reason we do not have more switch hitters is so few players think about doing it. There are advantages to switch hitting. Point out to your players those advantages. Your players do so many things, with their left hand, most can therefore learn to switch hit. Practice hitting badminton birds, using a batting tee or hit with the soft toss drill. Not all will take to the challenge. But some will, to their advantage.

♦   ♦   ♦   ♦   ♦

Unfortunately, coaches are going to have to keep batting averages. The media and some recruiters might want them. Too many times batting averages are inaccurate and thus meaningless. A more meaningful and important statistic is the On Base Average. A player does not have to get a base hit to be credited for getting "on base." Except for forcing out a runner, a player should receive credit for getting "on base" by way of an error, walk, hit by a pitch, a base hit, or a missed third strike that he beats out the throw to first, etc. Providing an On Base Average, versus a batting average, gives a player a more positive team attitude. All players now have a feeling that they are making an offensive contribution to the team's effort to win ball games. Team spirit is re-enforced.

8

FIELDING AND THROWING FUNDAMENTALS

Frequently, we label a player as not having "soft hands." Not so. All of your players have "soft hands." To demonstrate that indisputable fact, simply throw them a raw egg. They will reach out and, with cupped hands, begin to receive the egg. Their hands "give" and gently pull the egg to their body, much like a funnel receives the water and funnels the water into the spout. Treat every ball as a raw egg and you find all of your players have "soft hands." "Reach" and "give" with the ball before the ball reaches the receiver's hands. Upon contact, the receiver brings the ball to his body in one fluid motion.

This change in nomenclature will not be easy. We have used the expressions, "catch the ball" and "play catch" so long, it's hard to use the word "receive," as in "let's play receive." Receiving the ball correctly must be practiced!!! Remember, receiving the egg and so it is with receiving the ball. Reach and give.

◆   ◆   ◆   ◆   ◆

A must fundamental; the receiver must watch the ball go into his glove!!! Too many misplayed thrown balls, grounders, pop ups and outfield fly balls occur because a player lifts his head just before receiving the ball. A couple of terms will help to remind your players ensure that your player is watching the ball into his glove:

♦ Just before receiving the ball, think, bob the head into the glove or

♦ Bite the ball into the glove.

Receive every ball with two hands. Otherwise, valuable time is lost in transferring the ball from the glove to the throwing hand. During that time consuming transfer, the base runner is doing just that...running. Insisting that players use both hands to receive a ball will not be easy. Players are used to using just their glove hand to receive a ball. But, they will learn when no other options are offered.

♦ ♦ ♦ ♦ ♦

A must drill for all players!!! To practice dropped balls, players should practice dropping the ball and picking it up with the bare hand. Players all too often pick up a ball off the ground with their glove hand. Bad technique. Pick the ball up with the bare hand, watching the ball go into the hand. By picking the ball up this way, time is saved. The ball transfer to the throwing hand is avoided, perhaps saving enough time to prevent a base runner from advancing. Players have to be drilled in this technique. It cannot be taken for granted by the coach. While picking up the ball, an important point to be emphasized is that the player's weight must be on the balls of the feet. Otherwise, just before picking up the ball, the player will rock back on his heels, thereby increasing the chances of not picking up the ball securely.

◆   ◆   ◆   ◆   ◆

Onto another team fundamental: the pitcher covering first on balls hit to his right and fielded by the first baseman. The pitcher breaks for first by getting to a point alongside the base line about 10 feet from the bag. Once this point is reached, the pitcher stays on the inside of the baseline towards the diamond and never crosses that line in his run to the base. Once the base is reached, the pitcher receives the ball and bounces towards centerfield (towards the second baseman's fielding position) to avoid any chance of a collision with the runner coming down the line.

In covering first on throws from the middle infielders (following the first baseman's throw to the second base bag to complete the "get one twice" double play), the pitcher receives the throw, not the second baseman. Again, just as in the play where the pitcher covers first on a throw from the first baseman, he runs to a spot 10 feet from the base and stays inside the foul line to receive the throw. Avoiding a collision with the runner is a must!!!

◆   ◆   ◆   ◆   ◆

In the force at second, whether the shortstop or second baseman takes the force throw, have the player use just the left foot on the bag. This technique eliminates confusion in the players mind about his footwork.

Receive the ball with the left foot on the base. Then, "crow hop" either across the bag or stepping back from the bag. To aid in the throw, infielders should open up, if possible, to avoid throwing across locked hips.

♦　♦　♦　♦　♦

Tag outs at the bases must be practiced. Infielders, give the runner a place to go. Straddle the base. Take the throw and put it between the base and the sliding runner with the ball held in the glove. The fielder's eyes must be on the spot of the tag. Let the runner tag himself out.

The catcher has a different mechanic for blocking the plate when tagging a runner. He should place his left heel on the point of the plate nearest third base. That gives the runner a side of the plate in which to slide. It also indicates to the catcher where the slide will take place. The right leg is extended out to the throw. Tag and roll out of the way in preparation for the next play. This is no time for bravery by forcing a collision at the plate. Bravery takes place when the batter stands in against the pitcher.

♦　♦　♦　♦　♦

This throwing drill is an early season must. Bad throws will always happen, no matter the level of baseball being played. They take place many times because a player throws the ball no matter what grip he has on the ball. But, we can improve throwing accuracy by making sure of a proper grip on the ball. To assure proper gripping, have your players toss the ball in the air and, upon reception, look to place two fingers across the double

62

seams. After a while, have the player adjust the ball to this position without looking at the ball. Soon the proper grip becomes automatic. However, it must be practiced constantly. Just don't take gripping the ball for granted!!!

♦   ♦   ♦   ♦   ♦

The thrower must step directly to his target. Too often a player will throw while not stepping in a line direct to his target.

♦   ♦   ♦   ♦   ♦

Players understand the proper mechanics for throwing a ball because most of them have pitched darts to a dart board. With a dart, the thrower has a target, the bull's eye. Your players must have a bull's eye when throwing a ball. The coach determines what the bull's eye is. My bull's eye was always the face of the receiver. Pick the belt buckle, numbers, bill of cap, whatever, just so they are throwing at a specific target. ALL throws are directed at that target. Catcher throwing to a base; outfielders throwing to cut-off men; infielders throwing to the first basemen. Think face, throw to the face. Concentration must be total. One doesn't throw to the first basemen. One throws to the first baseman's face.

Back to the dart board pitch. Once the dart is pitched, one continues to focus on the bull's eye during the entire flight of the dart. One doesn't pitch and immediately look away. When throwing a baseball, how often have we seen players turn their heads? Focusing on the target, imaging or picturing the ball finding the target must be recognized for an accurate throw. It is important that the player see his ball all the way to the target.

♦   ♦   ♦   ♦   ♦

A good mechanic is to throw down on the ball. The hand must be on top of the ball. The follow through must be down, as if the ball was being thrown to the ground. The follow through action must be severe. You can't just drop the arm after the ball is released. The way to remember this technique is to keep throwing after the ball is released.

9

CATCHING

With men on base, your catcher should move back from the plate about six inches to give him a bit more room to "pour" himself into his throws to any base. With men on base, the pitched ball must be received with two hands. Receiving the ball with one hand is unacceptable. The catcher's throw must be imagined to the face of the receiver. Again, on every pitch catchers must think as if the runner(s) is going to steal. Coaching point: Speed of getting a throw off is as important as a strong arm.

♦　♦　♦　♦　♦

For the catcher, some things you must do with runners on bases:

♦ Receive the ball with two hands.

♦ Facilitate getting rid of the ball quickly when runners attempt to steal.

♦ Move back from the batter six to eight inches, making possible a strong "crow hop" move when throwing. It also makes it possible for you to lean into the pitch. In effect, the move is the beginning of your throw, before the pitched ball is received. By putting your weight on the forward foot, you are already into your "crow hop."

- Before your throw, do not rise to a standing position. This wastes time. Throw from your sitting position and go into your "crow hop," moving toward the base being thrown to. Quickness of a ball release is more important than a strong arm in gunning down base stealers.

- Always look at the runners before throwing the ball back to your pitcher.

- Do not loop your return throw to your pitcher. Runners can steal a base on a rainbow throw to the pitcher.

- Your pitch signals must be concealed. Make sure you have a coach check them frequently.

- See to it that your pitcher stays focused. He must be interested in all your signals.

- Make certain that your pitcher knows your pitch-out signal and that he knows how to execute it.

- On throws to second on attempted steals, throw when you see a middle infielder break to cover the base. Your cue to throw to second is the infielder moving, not seeing the runner going. Infielder moves to cover---you throw!!!

- Throwing to third base, you will be able to see the runner move immediately. That is your cue to throw to third.

♦ On cut-off throws from the outfielders, it is your responsibility to direct your first or third baseman where they throw the ball. They depend upon you for instructions.

♦ On pop ups, whether fair or foul, locate the ball before you discard your mask. Then, toss it well away from your path to the ball. Then get under the ball, so that if you miss it---it will hit you on the forehead.

♦ When no runners are on the bases, you may receive the pitched ball in your crouch position. When runners are on base, you must rise up to a sitting position (getting in a throwing position) to receive the pitched ball.

10

OFFENSIVE STRATEGY

If you are going to sacrifice bunt, the batter must square <u>before</u> the pitcher releases the ball. The runner doesn't advance until he sees the bunt is down.

If the pitch is a bad pitch to bunt, you can run and bunt with the batter not offering. If this happens, you simply have a straight steal taking place.

◆ ◆ ◆ ◆ ◆

As for the squeeze bunt (a good play), the batter squares around <u>after</u> the pitcher releases the ball. The squeeze bunt must be hidden as long as possible. If the play is on, the batter must attempt the bunt no matter where the pitch is. The runner holds until the pitch is delivered and then he takes off for home.

◆ ◆ ◆ ◆ ◆

Stealing home is a play that depends upon the defense not doing its job. First of all, the runner does not return to his base following the pitch. The catcher fails to check the runner who has a lead from his previous lead-off. The pitcher fails to look at the runner during his wind-up. With these factors in place, the runner takes off during the pitcher's wind-up. The batter holds his position in the batter's box until the pitch crosses the plate and then moves out of the way enabling the runner to have room to make his slide. A risky play, but it can be accomplished if these defensive mistakes are observed. Don't attempt this play unless it is practiced in the team fundamentals part of your practice.

♦　♦　♦　♦　♦

With runners on first and third, or with runners on second and third, you very often can score that runner on a ground ball to the infield. Just have the runner go home on contact. Automatic. It eliminates the runner's hesitation whether to attempt to score. If he is thrown out at home, you have not lost all that much. You still end up with a runner in scoring position. By going on contact, you force the defense to make a play they ordinarily do not make, throwing home to get a runner. A good play, use it!!!

11

BASE RUNNING

The ways to cause trouble on game day are countless: mechanical errors, mental lapses, poor responses in the batter's box, judgment mistakes by the coaching staff to name just a few. Add to this list...base running mistakes. Base running errors might just head the list of costly errors leading to negative game results.

Once a runner is on base treat him as you would a priceless gem. Runs happen ONLY because a team has players on the bases. It is difficult enough to get players on base without losing them by foolish, undisciplined, careless non-thinking activity.

♦ ♦ ♦ ♦ ♦

To illustrate how things can go wrong when running the bases, a recent high school game is referred to. Close game in which the outcome was directly related to base running mistakes:

♦ Runner on second, picked off by a catcher's throw.

♦ Runner on second, picked off by the pitcher. In the ensuing run-down the runner on first failed to advance to second.

♦ Runner on third failed to go on ball-bat contact and was thrown out in a close play at home. Coach on third gave clear instructions to the runner as to what to do on such contact. Runner hesitated and was out.

♦ Runner on second attempts to score on a hit to the outfield. Runner thrown out at home only because he didn't slide. His help via the next hitter was negligible, no animated indication as to what the runner was to do.

Costly mistakes, two sure runs resulted in two outs at home. Doesn't have to happen and shouldn't happen!!!

♦ ♦ ♦ ♦ ♦

When attempting to beat out an infield hit, keep your all out running speed going until the base has been crossed. It is fundamental that the batter run through the base.

♦ ♦ ♦ ♦ ♦

Coaching point: Once a player reaches a base, have him hold something in either hand (dirt, a pebble, batting gloves) so the runner has a closed hand grip. By holding an object, the sliding runner will throw his hands up, thus avoiding breaking his slide with his hands that lead to hand, finger, wrist, elbow or shoulder injuries. Holding an object is the key. The fist will stay closed by doing so.

♦ ♦ ♦ ♦ ♦

Lead-offs. Runners do not lead-off until the pitcher places his foot on the pitching rubber. The "hidden ball trick" is now eliminated. At that point, the pitcher must have the ball or it is a balk.

When leading off, use the slide steps. No crossing of the legs!!!

By the crossing your legs, you are inviting the pitcher to pick you off while you are "crossed." Then, with a glide step (not a cross over step) the runner takes his preliminary lead. Such lead is taken with the runner sure that no matter what the pitcher does, he will be able to return to the base safely.

Once the pitcher delivers the ball, the secondary lead takes place, again with a slide step. This lead to be taken directly between the lead-off base and the next base.

The steal takes place once the runner determines that the pitch will be delivered to the catcher (point of pitcher's shoulder nearest home plate will indicate the direction of the pitch, attempted pick-off or deliver to the catcher).

The first step in stealing may be either a cross over step or a direct step. Both ways are acceptable. It is important that the first steps be quick and the body stays low (witness the start of a sprinters race). Just don't come up to a near erect position too soon. In every sense of the word you are a sprinter. Your only goal is reaching the next base as quickly as you can.

Don't look for the ball. Just go all out and end up with a slide. Once you are determined to slide, then do it. Don't change your mind at the last second (sure fire way to get hurt).

♦ ♦ ♦ ♦ ♦

Once on second, the usual caution must be observed...where are the middle infielders, does the pitcher have the ball? No "hidden ball" embarrassment out can take place if you hold to the base until the pitcher steps on the pitching rubber. Your lead-off doesn't take place until that happens.

Take the preliminary lead and hold it. Just know you can get back to the base, no matter the fakes of the infielders or a throw from the pitcher. Hold that preliminary lead no matter the actions of the middle infielders. Bouncing back and forth to the base is wasted effort and makes it possible for the pitcher to deliver the ball to the batter when the runner has a negligible lead off. Going back to the base certainly decreases the chances of a safe steal and puts in jeopardy a possible score on a single.

Rule for the runner on second: on a ground ball hit ahead of you to either the third baseman or in the hole to the shortstop, stay; on a ball hit behind you, come. Come on the throw to first by the third baseman and the shortstop.

♦ ♦ ♦ ♦ ♦

Lead-off from third differently from other bases. Down in foul territory and back in fair. Down in foul to nullify getting hit by a fair ball resulting in an out. Coming back in fair territory makes it a difficult throw for the catcher. Once the primary lead is taken and the pitcher delivers to the plate, turn and walk towards home plate. Walking enables the runner to get a great start on ground balls to the infield if a score is to be attempted.

◆　◆　◆　◆　◆

And now for plays at home plate. The next batter must take on the responsibilities of a coach. Whether the runner is to slide or stand up is determined by the next batter/coach. Signals making this determination must be animated. Body language is most important. There must be no question in the runner's mind what he is to do in this situation.

◆　◆　◆　◆　◆

No matter what base the runner is on, he must be aware that on every pitch the possibility exists that the catcher will attempt to pick him off. When the pitch passes the plate, get back to your base IN A HURRY!!! Nothing kills a rally, nor deflates a team more, than a runner being picked off by the catcher.

◆　◆　◆　◆　◆

Coaches, your responsibilities are many and vital. Base runners must know what your signals mean. Practice those signals: when to run through first base, when to make the turn at first base and when to go to second. Runners must know, through practice, the signals for standing up going into third or sliding into third; the signal for rounding third and going on to score. Correct base running must not be taken for granted.

First base coach determines whether a runner is to run through the bag or make a turn and hold, or make a turn and continue on to second. Coach...the runner is yours and what he does is all your responsibility!!!

The third base coach is totally responsible for what a runner does because, for the most part, the ball is behind the runner, out of sight by the runner. Whether the runner is to slide, stand-up (going into third) or is to continue on to home is solely the coach's responsibility. The runner is entirely dependent upon your judgment.

◆　◆　◆　◆　◆

Base running must be practiced, just as hitting, throwing and fielding must be practiced. And it can be. Use the drill previously mentioned, the "situation" drill, where your starting team stays at bat vs. slow pitching until 15-18 outs are made. Now, coach, you will have real game situations taking place and real base running decisions will be practiced.

◆　◆　◆　◆　◆

Throughout the season, give time to sliding practice. Three lines going at the same time. Practice at only one base cuts down the number of slides a player makes in the practice time allotted.

Do not permit head first slides!!! By eliminating the head first slide, head or neck or spine injury can be avoided. Use only the bent leg straight slide.

When in doubt, slide!!! Slide with no hesitation. Complete the slide and avoid injuries!!!

12

DEFENSIVE STRATEGY

On a steal of second, your players must know who is to cover second. I have only the shortstop covering second. You may disagree with that, but it works for me and avoids confusion.

The catcher throws to second the instant he sees his shortstop breaking for the bag. The catcher need not see the runner attempting the steal. Shortstop moves, the catcher throws. Again, imagine the face of the receiver and get the ball to that spot.

The catcher can see the runner stealing third because his vision is in line with the runner's lead-off position. Runner goes, catcher throws. On a steal, base men should straddle the base they are covering. The ball and glove are placed in front of the bag, so the runner really tags himself out.

◆　◆　◆　◆　◆

With a runner on any base, the pitcher has the responsibility of making the runner stop before the pitch is delivered. This rule holds true for any lead-off of any base. Pitchers <u>must</u> make the runners stop before delivering the ball.

And, catchers, with men on base, check the runners before throwing back to the pitcher. Throw hard, never a looping throw back to the pitcher with runners on base.

◆　◆　◆　◆　◆

With a man on first, the bunt coverage is the same as if no runners are on base. <u>Important:</u> with a man on first and the third baseman fielding the bunt, the catcher must cover third. This is the only time a catcher leaves home plate when runners are on base.

With a runner on second, the charge to cover the bunt is changed. The third baseman covers his base, while the pitcher and first baseman angle their charge to, in effect, cover territory covered as though the third baseman was involved.

Suggestion: forget trying to force the runner at second on a fielded bunt. The attempt is botched too many times, resulting in runners advancing and no outs achieved.

On throws to first with the catcher fielding the bunt, the throw must be inside the first baseline. On missed third strikes, the catcher's throw must be outside the first baseline. The rule: don't cross a baseline with a throw.

◆　◆　◆　◆　◆

A "must" team fundamental is throws from the outfield. Cut-off throws must be face high. Cut-off infielders must receive the throw over their throwing shoulder.

80

One of your infielders must be in a position to direct the cut-off infielders throw.

Cut-off players get your hands up so the outfielders have a clear target to throw at. Upon reception of the ball, "follow the glove" rule takes over. The ball must be caught (received) with both hands in order to save time transferring the ball to the throwing hand.

A practice drill that involves all three outfielders throwing to bases at the same time will keep all of your outfielders active and will eliminate boredom. One outfielder throws to one base, another to another base, while the third outfielder throws to a third base. Outfielders then change the base to be thrown to.

◆　◆　◆　◆　◆

Infielders are responsible for relaying the number of outs to the outfielders. I suggest the shortstop tells the left fielder and center fielder, the second baseman tells the right fielder. Such communication is a must.

13

GAME DAY

For youth baseball fans from T-ball through high school (and fans include players, parents, grandparents, coaches), rarely have I seen unsportsman like displays of conduct. Little attention or publicity is given to positive behavior. But, let an unfortunate incident occur (heated arguments, physical negative behavior between players, coaches and parents) and the story makes headlines. The few, the very few, sully the behavior of the many.

Coaches must remember that behavior, whether positive or negative, is totally established by your conduct. You, with a proper attitude, will set the standard of sportsmanship for your fans and your players.

♦　♦　♦　♦　♦

As for your deportment relative to your players, the opposing players, the opposing manager and the umpire, just pause before getting overly excited and take the time to realize who you are dealing with. Certainly not accomplished ball players, so accept and understand mistakes. You just can't afford to get caught up in the philosophy that "winning is everything." Your players will not get a hit every time at bat or field cleanly every ball or make every throw an accurate one. Such is not done even by the best of major league players.

83

Getting involved in heated arguments with an opposing manager is simply not justified. You have enough to do just giving your undivided attention to your own players, which leaves you no time to get mixed up with an opposing manager or players. Be there for your players and leave those on the other bench alone.

♦ ♦ ♦ ♦ ♦

As for umpires, just accept the fact that decisions will not always go your way. A poor call on your batter will happen. A missed play at a base will happen. After all, we aren't dealing with big league professional umpires.

Umpires don't stop games to yell at your pitcher for failing to get the ball over the plate or your batters for failing to hit the ball. No umpire will embarrass a player by making fun of him following a fielding error or after a throwing error. That umpire deserves the same kind of respect from you.

Baseball is a game of mistakes. Accept them and move on to the next play. If your players were perfect, they wouldn't be playing for you. If umpires were perfect, they wouldn't be doing your youth league games.

♦ ♦ ♦ ♦ ♦

Again, your players will reflect your attitude, your example and your display of sportsmanship in game situations. If you stomp and rave and become argumentative, your players and fans will follow suit. Teaching young people positive values through the medium of baseball is your primary responsibility. If you win games via that approach, fine. If not, that is also acceptable. It just could be that your players aren't as accomplished baseball wise as the opposing players.

♦   ♦   ♦   ♦   ♦

Cheer for your team and not against your opponent.

♦   ♦   ♦   ♦   ♦

Bench "housekeeping" is a must to create an attitude that this game is important. It is a part of playing good baseball. Your players must know that all phases of the game are important to you. You, the coach, set the example!!!

Bench deportment means players sitting on the bench, not spread out all over the grounds. Strive for a climate of doing things right while not on the field. Players must watch the game. Players must be aware of what is going on. NO visiting with friends or parents behind the fence. If players are going to play the game, they must immerse themselves in the proper involvement with that game. Bench deportment comes under this heading.

Uniforms must be worn your way, coach. Individual player expressions are derived by the way a player plays the game, not from his version of wearing his uniform. Looking sloppy equates to playing the game sloppy. A clean uniform for every game and that uniform is worn your way.

♦   ♦   ♦   ♦   ♦

Certainly players should have "fun" playing the game, but not the kind of "fun" enjoyed from a Sunday softball game in the park. "Fun" must come from an organized team and from playing the game with the pursuit of executing baseball skills perfectly. Playing the game properly must be important to your players. It must be important to your players to field balls cleanly, to make proper and good throws. Eliminating offensive and defensive mistakes must be a high priority to your players.

◆ ◆ ◆ ◆ ◆

You will lose games simply because the opposition is better. There's little you can do about that. Do not dwell on such a game. Just move on.

14

LASTING IMPRINTS
TO PLAYERS AND COACHES

TO PLAYERS

To you, aspiring baseball players from eight to eighteen; just remember the way to becoming a good baseball player is to practice and practice and practice your baseball fundamentals. Whether you practice or not is up to you. Just know that wishing to become a decent ball player will not cut it!!! You can't "wish" for skill improvement!!! Improvement will come only from practice...repetition. Repetition is the key. Become one of the few who will pay the price of constant practice.

Tennis ball against a wall (garage door), hitting off a tee in your basement, hitting badminton birds in your backyard, engaging in a supervised weight program (strength is IMPORTANT)...these things can be done and should be done the year round.

You want to make your youth team, your high school team? Well, DO IT!!! Pay attention to your coach and resolve to yourself to MEET THE CHALLENGE of becoming a baseball player...so, don't talk baseball, or wish baseball...PRACTICE baseball!!!

◆　◆　◆　◆　◆

87

Think of a baseball field as a blank canvas. Each player, by his baseball actions and his movements, paints his own pictures on that field canvas. Totally original. No one EVER made the same steps in the same way on the ball field. A ball diamond is not just a field. It provides a setting to make something original, an area where a work of art can be accomplished.

◆　◆　◆　◆　◆

Some thoughts addressed to players from youth leagues through the high school years. You have just lost a game that eliminates you from a league championship or a pursuit of a State championship...but you still have games to play. Make certain that you don't lose your interest in those games still to be played.

Pursue the next game with its challenges. Each game has its own identity, its own rewards both from an individual standpoint and from a team standpoint. Playing such games with dulled enthusiasm fails you, your team and the game of baseball.

◆　◆　◆　◆　◆

Meet the challenge of every game with total effort. Anything less is an affront to your considerable physical and mental gifts. Said gifts are never to be taken for granted. Even though a game comes under the heading of being a non-descript game, i.e., no championship involved, few people in the stands, not even a line score in the local paper, that game has meaning to YOU. So, honor that meaning and that game with your best doing, your best effort. No matter the importance of a game, leave the field following the game with the thought...this is who I am!!! The good player, the exceptional player is one that plays hard with so few people knowing that such a game is ever being played. Anyone can get excited about a "big" game. The challenge is to play with total effort whether the game is a "big" one or not. Play with this kind of an attitude and you will have little difficulty playing well in the "big" games. Earn the right to play well in such games and that "right" will fall into place. Each practice, each ground ball fielded in practice done perfectly, and with a desire to do things right, will lead to good things for you when the time comes to play well in a needed situation. Baseball is demanding and the game will know when you have cut corners, mentally and physically.

◆　◆　◆　◆　◆

Each game has its own importance!!! Will you always successfully meet the demands of a game? Of course not! But you can walk away from such games knowing that game was respected by you. The best feeling in the world is to sit in the locker room and, whether a win or a loss, to say to yourself, I did my best. And then, the next day walk out on the ball field prepared to give effort all over again. Not always easy, but no one has said baseball is easy. Just be true to the game, your coach, your teammates and to yourself. By doing so...you have honored a great game and have brought honor to yourself.

◆　◆　◆　◆　◆

Enjoy the physical and mental demands of your age. You will be able to run as you do, be able to move as you can, be able to get excited about a game for a very short time in your life. So, don't pass up the opportunity to challenge your gifts during this time. Leave yourself on the field. By doing that you will be able to look back with no regrets. Do what you can...NOW!!!

The game has been with us for a long time. Just make sure when you are finished playing that you are one who refused to back down from the challenge of playing the game well!!! Pursue the win of this game. Approach the game as if it is to be the last game you'll ever play. You have no way of knowing that it just might be that, so give each opportunity your very best shot!!!

♦   ♦   ♦   ♦   ♦

TO COACHES

Coach, your team will take on the personality of YOU!!! Your behavior will be your team's behavior. Your intensity (players aware that a practice or game is important to you) will become important to them. YOU WILL SEND A MESSAGE TO YOUR PLAYERS AS TO HOW YOU WANT THE GAME OR PRACTICE TO DEVELOP. You are the leader, so lead!!!

Coach, you have a passion for the game, a major component relative to your ability to coach the game of baseball. Your players will catch that passion and, in turn, they will play the game with passion. Once you lose the passion that the game be played right, it is time to think about getting out of coaching. This passion never varies, whether you are 20-0 or 0-20. A poor team deserves your best shot, just as you would give a good team your best effort!!!

♦   ♦   ♦   ♦   ♦

ATTITUDE IS EVERYTHING!!! Players must think: I am a good ball player; I am a good hitter; I am a good fielder. And you Coach, must re-enforce that attitude. Don't permit your players to think less of themselves as ball players. Players must never give up the thought that they are good ball players in all facets of the game!!!

♦   ♦   ♦   ♦   ♦

Coach, explore the world of IMAGING, the use of the mental to facilitate the physical. Picture hitting line drives. Picture proper fielding form. By imagining proper baseball skill form, you will go a long way in perfecting proper mechanics, in fielding and in hitting and a player's overall baseball skills. There is much literature available that will acquaint you with imaging. Books by Mazwell Maltz will get you started. Begin this fascinating subject with Maltz's book, *Psycho Cybernetics*, and go on from there.

♦   ♦   ♦   ♦   ♦

The printed sign says:

OPPORTUNITYISNOWHERE and your players will read it just that way: OPPORTUNITY IS NOWHERE. Then, ask them to study the words carefully. One of your players will come up with a different read that will go like this: OPPORTUNITY IS NOW HERE. Big difference. One that has important meaning to your players. Life is only once, so take advantage of the NOW.

◆   ◆   ◆   ◆   ◆

Do not be afraid of losing. Winning is what you are playing games for, but you are not always going to win. No matter the game results, you can ALWAYS have a "good" team. Proper execution of plays is a desired objective, but such results are not always possible. Baseball is not an easy game to play. The pursuit of excellence should be what a team and coach should be after. You cannot dilute or compromise your standards in order to win a game. You will gain total respect from your players for such an attitude.

◆   ◆   ◆   ◆   ◆

Trust yourself. Your approach to teaching the game may well be an improvement over all else read or listened to in clinics. Use this information and those ideas advanced here as a reference point for your way of coaching.

Enjoy your coaching experience!!! A great way to add dimension to your life.

◆   ◆   ◆   ◆   ◆

Finally, the most important aspect of coaching or playing is called ENTHUSIASM. Neither you, nor your players, can buy it or steal it or get it by wishing. Your players can get it ONLY from you. You possess this precious commodity and your players will emulate it. Enthusiasm must come from you first. Just do not expect your players to exhibit enthusiasm unless you have it!!! If you possess and exhibit enthusiasm and your players will mirror your attitude to the game. From YOU to THEM. No other way!!!

Will enthusiasm assure you a winning season? No! You need good pitching for that, but it will ensure you have a "good" competitive team. You will be associated with a group of highly motivated players. With enthusiasm, you will enjoy coaching spirited players. They will reward you with their desire to learn and compete. Who could ask for anything more?

Above all else, do not ever lose your ENTHUSIASM for teaching the game of baseball. Enthusiasm will cover a lot of mistakes on your part!!!

◆　◆　◆　◆　◆

Now it is up to you, Coach, to develop your players into decent youth league and high school ball players. This progress can happen...only by teaching skills, not yelling skills. Teach, don't yell! Kids will learn if given a chance through your patience.

◆　◆　◆　◆　◆

Coaches and players, baseball is a great game backed by a rich history. You join the many that have played and loved the game. Welcome aboard!!! Pay your respects to the game and its traditions by doing your best at every opportunity to play. Play the game with energy and a quest to do your best at all times.

UNIVERSITY SCHOOL

Athletic Department

Dunno the date

Neddrow...

A contribution to your words to live by...and I realize
you didn't ask for my in put...I write and submit anyway...

My idea of the only obsensity I know...those othr words
classified as obsenities...just words...uncouth...lousy
way to espress oneself...

My wordis...WHEN...people live by that word...I'll
be happy...WHEN...I'll find contentment...WHEN...things will
be better...WHEN...we live out lives not in the now but in
the WHEN...such comes and goes and we still involved in the
concept of just wait until...WHEN...meanwhile the NOW is passing
us by...

Just thought you ought to know...

Blessings a-plenty,

V. M.

UPPER SCHOOL · 2785 S.O.M. CENTER ROAD · HUNTING VALLEY, OHIO · 44022
(216) 831-2200 · FAX (216) 292-7811 · www.upper.us.edu   Recycled and Recyclable

15

FRED HEINLEN - THE MAN
AS EXPERIENCED AND REMEMBERED

Ned Grossman
Shaker Heights High School - Class of 1961
BBA, MBA - Case Western Reserve University
President, Grossman Consulting, LLC. Cleveland, Ohio
President, Diamond Publishing Company, Cleveland, Ohio

I first met Fred Heinlen in 1951. I was eight years old and in the second grade. After school during the basketball season, I would ride my bicycle to the high school gym and shoot baskets while the Varsity was practicing. I vividly remember Fred coming over to me, this "half-pint" kid (I eventually "filled out" at 5'5"!) shooting hook shots and complimenting me on my form. He knew I had no chance of becoming a Shaker Varsity basketball player, but 50 years later, I still cherish the memory of the venerable high school coach taking time to praise and encourage a random eight year old "wanna be."

In the spring of 1959, I was a sophomore on Shaker's Junior Varsity baseball team. The Board of Education saw fit to non-renew the contracts of two very popular teachers. The students were upset and staged an after school support demonstration. Most of the students weren't really interested in the two teachers, but were attracted by the TV cameras. (Remember, this was 1959, before the student demonstration filled 60's.) The curious baseball team attended the rally, thus reporting late to baseball practice. Coach Heinlen was seething! He heatedly made it abundantly clear that we were

97

either demonstrators or baseball players. On that day, we had chosen to be demonstrators, i.e. NO PRACTICE!

By the end of my senior year, I had completed a most mediocre high school baseball career. At the annual spring sports awards, it was the custom for Coach Heinlen to say a few parting words about each player. Fred always had the knack of making his players, even the mediocre ones, feel important and worthwhile. To me, a journeyman, he said: "Neddy, you contributed. You will be missed." Those typical Fred succinct, simple words of praise have given me unforgettable satisfaction and inspiration to this day.

In 1965, as a Case Western Reserve University senior, I had no afternoon classes and asked Fred about being a volunteer assistant baseball coach. Fortunately for me, Fred accepted. Four events remain vivid recollections:

♦ Our dinner at Keifer's restaurant the night before the "draw" for the sectional tournament. We felt like major league executives preparing our strategies for the all-important playoffs.

♦ The rather meaningless game Shaker played the day before leaving for the State tournament in Columbus. We were well ahead in the late innings. On a routine force play, our runner failed to slide into second. Fred was irate at the lack of player's hustle and the failure to follow fundamentals. The runner spent the rest of the game on the bench. Play the game properly or sit! The offender was Shaker's All-State Shortstop, Rodd Heinlen---Fred's son. Everyone was treated the same---no favorites.

♦ Fred had arranged for our team to practice at the Upper Arlington High School field in Columbus the day before the semi-final game. As we got off our bus, the Upper Arlington team practice halted. All their eyes were rivoted on the heralded Shaker players as they walked to their practice field. The Upper Arlington player's unstated admiration and respect gave an immeasurable boost of confidence to all our players.

♦ Being part of a State Championship team---a winning combination of great kids, excellent players, supportive parents and above all, an inspirational coach whose hard work, motivation and leadership made it happen.

But Fred's most important contribution to Ned Grossman was as a long-time close friend and mentor. After college, I was a floundering youth who had no idea what he really wanted to do with his life. Fred was always there for me---and I mean always. For several years, I spent countless evenings in Fred's living room talking baseball and being counseled. One day Fred gave me a set of Earl Nightengale audio cassette tapes: *"Lead The Field."*

I agreed to listen, not because I thought a set of tapes could solve a person's problems and put him on the road to success, but as a favor to Fred. I naively thought if the path to success were spelled out in a set of tapes, why wouldn't everyone listen? Why wasn't everyone successful? Well, those tapes were the turning point for me. They provided the necessary logic, understanding, purpose and direction for success, happiness and achievement.

Fred's unselfish interest, time, understanding, love and patience are responsible for putting me on the right path. Those wonderful evening chats, while not as frequent, still continue and are cherished.

Thanks Fred. Thanks for everything!

Dave Albright
University School, Class of 1988

Miami University
Vice President, Keystone Components, Twinsburg, Ohio

I was fortunate enough to play for Coach Heinlen during the mid-late 1980's at University School. There are numerous comical stories about Coach Heinlen, many that I share with other former athletes and no one can compete with a good Coach Heinlen story. From our JV football defensive signals where Coach would yell from the sideline, "left linebacker blitz," to his dressing down of a JV basketball teammate of mine with the observation that he had "the body of a forty year old fat man."

Coach Heinlen was tough, anyone who has met the man knows that. As a challenge to get our uniforms for freshman baseball we had to bench press our weight. Coach didn't leave us to fend for ourselves, he challenged himself to bench press 200 pounds, and at the age of 70, he did it.

Three years later, as a senior, I was dealt the misfortune of a knee injury in the first game of our football season. After reconstructive surgery to repair two torn ligaments I set my goal to be prepared for the upcoming baseball season. I spent every night after school rehabilitating in the pool and weight room while my teammates were out on the playing fields. Coach Heinlen was always there with support and encouragement for me. He'd check on my progress, show his concern and interest. When I eventually made it to the gym for laps, he'd frequently pass me (while doing his own regimen) and pass along positive thoughts every time around. His encouragement helped me through a very difficult period in my life. His concern for a young man who needed some strength is something I'll never forget and always be grateful for. I did, in fact, achieve my goal and made it back in time for baseball in the spring. Looking back I realize that the

100

support to help a young man achieve this goal was more important than the goal itself.

When I think of Coach Heinlen, I think of a guy who would ride his players to the edge of their thresholds, but when one of his young men needed to be built back up, he was there for you. I treasure my years with Coach Heinlen.

Robert Elton
Shaker Heights High School - Class of 1950
U.S. Military Academy
BS, MS - University of Virginia
Retired Lieutenant General, U.S. Army

Fred came into my life right after WWII. He graduated from Springfield College in Massachusetts and served in the Army Air Corps. My father had also served in the Air Corps so there was instant camaraderie. In his dealings with young men, he was always testing character. He knew that he was not perfect, but he tried to instill in his players that, in the life they would lead following baseball, there would be several challenges that would call upon their values and character. He believed that it was his job to help us see the right way. In addition to teaching all week, he then put on a tie and taught the high school class at Sunday School (Plymouth Congregational Church of Shaker Heights).

Tom Comella

Shaker Heights High School - Class of 1955

Case Institute of Technology
Managing Editor, Machine Design Magazine,
    Penton Publishing Company, Cleveland, OH
Retired Group Physicist, Livermore Laboratory, Livermore, California

Fred Heinlen writing a book about coaching baseball: What a great idea! No one has more to say on the subject. If today's "professionals" had learned baseball from Fred, we would be watching a more interesting game and a higher quality of play.

I played centerfield for Fred Heinlen during Shaker's 1954 and 1955 seasons. I learned early that his approach to the game transcended baseball. He not only taught the fundamentals and strategy of the game better than anyone I know, he also understood that a player had to be fully engaged, mentally, in every moment of every game if he was to do his best and help his team the most.

But, above all, Fred Heinlen epitomized the qualities of character required to be a winner, in life as well as sports. Under his tutelage, a young man got lessons in self-control, hard work, courage, and tenacity under pressure, as well as baseball. Fred Heinlen didn't just coach baseball. He was a true Maestro of the Game!

My most vivid memory of playing for Fred was from the 1954 season. We were tied with Parma for the Lake Erie League Championship and had to play an elimination game at Shaker's field to determine which team would advance to the district tournament. The score was tied in the last half of the seventh inning. Leading off, I reached first base on an error. With one out, I stole second base. Then I stole third base. The crowd was going crazy. People were lined up and down the

102

sidelines, making Fred a little hard to see as I looked over to the first-base coaching box for instructions.

We had a few basic signals and in crucial situations like this one, those signals could only come from the Boss. But in the heat of the moment, with all the commotion, I couldn't make out what Fred was signaling. Besides, I never dreamed that he would want me to do anything but protect the potential winning run. So I kept my left foot firmly on third base.

Finally, with two outs, a frustrated Heinlen dispensed with the fancy hand movements. He waved his arms to get my attention, cupped his hands over his mouth, and yelled "C-O-M-E-L-L-A," while pointing toward home plate. I couldn't believe he wanted me to steal home. Ernie Lees, the Parma pitcher, started his windup when I took off for home plate, running for my life. As I started to slide, I heard the ball whizzing toward the catcher. The umpire yelled "SAFE!" We won the game!

Everyone was ecstatic. Everyone but Fred Heinlen. Always the teacher and seeker of perfection, he calmly walked over to me as I brushed the dirt from my uniform and told me, in that no-nonsense manner of his, that I had to work on reading signals.

I miss those days. I miss Fred Heinlen.

Jerry Goetz
Shaker Heights High School - Class of 1964
BA - University of Notre Dame
Professional Baseball Advisor

Fred Heinlen and I lived a mere two streets from one another. Fred played a significant role in my life and I transferred much of what I learned from him to my own son who is now a professional baseball player in the Florida Marlins organization. Some vivid remembrances immediately come to mind.

On the day President Kennedy was assassinated, school was canceled and most businesses were closed. Fred refused to cancel basketball practice. He put us through the toughest practice of the year. He said now was the time not only to mourn, but to work harder than we ever had to accomplish our goals. I never forgot that lesson.

Fred truly loves the game of baseball. On the weekends when we were growing up, Fred, his son Rodd, myself and anyone else who wanted to come (sometimes nobody else) would meet at the high school field and just "play baseball" for hours at a time. My passion for the game developed during those early years. It was never a burden, always fun.

"AS IF," "Of what value," etc. Fred would use these and other short phrases to convey strong messages during practices.

Rodd Heinlen (Son and Player)
Shaker Heights High School - Class of 1966

    BS - Florida State University
    B Architecture - University of Idaho
    Architect, Isle of Palm, South Carolina

Dad was always organizing summer baseball teams, primarily to keep his future high school teams playing together. When I was in seventh or eighth grade, maybe 13 years old, he got a group of us together to play in the Colt League. We would arrange practice time in the evenings on the diamond behind the old Onaway School. Needless to say, fields were at a premium and one hour, twice a week was about all we could hope for. One night we all show up for a 6:30 PM practice and another team is finishing up their scheduled time. As time passed, Dad said something to the other coach about them running over. We waited another ten or fifteen minutes as they continued to play on. Dad's patience began to wear thin and it wasn't long before he and the other coach started getting into it. We were all just standing around watching. Then their coach throws a punch and hit Dad right in the face. Dad stood there for a few seconds then said, "Hit me again. Hit me again if it makes you feel better." I suppose out of embarrassment the coach refused. Everyone just sort of stood there in silence. He left with his team. We left with our team. I was very proud that night to be Fred Heinlen's son.

Jim Humpel
Coach, Brush High School, Cleveland, Ohio 1964 - 1981
BA - Heidelberg College & John Carroll
Ohio High School Baseball Coach of Fame 1977

I became the Head Baseball Coach at Charles F. Brush High School in the 1964-65 school year and Fred's competitor in the Lake Erie League. In fact, we played Shaker Heights in the regional tournament that spring, losing to his team that eventually went on to win the State baseball championship.

It was after that game that we became friends and he my baseball mentor. We both coached summer teams in the same league. We met many times before games and would sit on a park bench and talk. It was during these conversations with Fred that my baseball coaching education really began. He would ask a question. I would answer and he would offer suggestions or alternatives. He truly helped me become a better coach.

One day, Shaker was to play at Euclid. The Shaker administration excused the team early from school to leave for the game. They did not give Fred early dismissal. The players went to the game; Fred did not. The game was not played. Fred always had a way of making his point!

Fred coached as many as four teams in the summer. He would often start a game, put his captain in charge, leave and go to another game. Only once did a team captain let him down by losing control and getting tossed. Fred called the umpire that same night and apologized to him for his teams' behavior. So did his captain!

His teams were always well-coached, disciplined, and competitive. I always looked forward to playing Shaker because we were competing against the best.

106

Neal Hesche
Shaker Heights High School - Class of 1948
BS, MBA - Kent State University
Physical Education Teacher, Coach & Acting Superintendent,
Berea High School, Cleveland, Ohio

Recently the phone rang at my house in Berea. "This is Fred Heinlen and I was driving along and I just thought about you coming out to practice at Shaker carrying all that catcher's equipment and so I decided to give you a call and say hello." What a surprise, after all these years.

During my sophomore year at Shaker, Coach Fred needed a catcher and asked if anyone wanted to try. I volunteered. So began a three year teaching experience for Fred and a learning experience for me. The lesson I remember most was when Coach Fred stayed after practice and hit "foul" balls straight up in the air to teach me how to catch this type of fly ball. He must have hit 100 to 150 balls. If you have ever tried to hit baseballs straight up in the air you know how difficult that is, and he wouldn't quit until I had mastered the techniques. Years later, I used the same techniques as the Berea High School Coach, and even had a former catcher tell me what a valuable lesson that was.

Fred was instrumental in getting the baseball coaches at Kent State University to take a look at me. As a result, I had three fine years on the Kent baseball team. He was always ready to help you get ahead in life. I thank him for all of his direction, support and help.

Scott Keller
Shaker Heights High School - Class of 1972
 BA - Yale University
 Principal, Dynamics Healthcare Advisors, Inc.

Fred is truly a unique man and has had a tremendous influence on my life. I think about him often. Whenever any of us who had the good fortune to play for him get together, it does not take long for us to re-tell (and re-live) the legendary stories about our time with Fred.

I remember one story in particular. A father simply couldn't help "coaching" his kid from the stands. Fred stopped the game, marched the kid up into the stands and sat him next to his father and said to the man, "Now we have to decide right now, are you coaching your boy or am I?...Because if you are, here is where he will sit for the remainder of the season!" Many years later, when Fred was coaching at University School, I remember talking to a friend of mine whose son was on the middle school team. She told me the exact same story and said that Fred must be old and senile. I assured her that he hadn't changed a bit! Her son ended up not pursuing baseball and became a champion swimmer.

By the time I was a senior, I overcame most of my fear of Fred and felt secure enough to ask him a tough question. I asked Fred why he picked 12 people in the ninth grade to play baseball for him, why he would not let more people on the team, or why he would not have tryouts after ninth grade? He explained that it didn't make sense to take a kid and have him sit on the bench for four years. Instead, the boy would be forced to pursue other interests. Fred said he may miss a few stars, but it was fair price to pay for all the other boys who found success in other ways than baseball. Baseball, like life, was meant to be played, not watched.

108

I have never run across anyone who was more devoted to a sport, hobby or occupation than Fred. I remember coming to practice and seeing Fred working on the field, picking up stones, raking the dirt. Running on and off the field, we had to fill up our gloves with stones. I remember playing at Yale for a coach who had a great professional career and coached in one of the best stadiums on the East Coast. But he didn't love the game like Fred did. I'd trade my entire Yale career for another ninth grade summer with Fred, playing baseball for four to five hours every day.

The rules were rigid...your behavior on and off the field fit to codified boundaries. Throwing to the right cut off man was an important as not smoking. The mistakes of the previous day were relived each day at noon. We started the day sitting on the bench. Fred would be walking up and own the length of the bench deep in thought. Sometimes fifteen minutes would go by without him saying a word. We would sit in complete silence hoping not to get singled out. Once Fred had spotted one of the players smoking in the neighborhood - he simply told the boy to go home - that was the end of his career. Tough medicine, but no one else ever thought of smoking.

The day I remember the most was the baseball awards ceremony after my senior year - the last time we got together as a team. Fred spoke about the season and each one of us. None of us saw it coming, but all of us broke down and cried. We simply didn't know how much Fred, baseball and each one of us had meant to each other.

Now, what I wish for my own boys is not so much to be on a championship team or win a bunch of awards. I want them to be taught by someone as devoted to his teachings as Fred, so they will understand that picking up rocks on a baseball field is as important as hitting a home run.

Roger Klein
Shaker Heights High School - Class of 1960

AB, MA, PhD - Dartmouth College, University of Chicago, Hebrew Union College
Associate Rabbi at The Temple, Tifereth Israel, Cleveland, Ohio
Adjunct Associate Professor, Family Medicine, Case Western Reserve School
    of Medicine

Upon returning to Cleveland with my wife and family in 1989, I read somewhere that Fred Heinlen was offering a clinic at Lomond School for young ballplayers. So I took my son, Danny, then age eight and a budding ball player, to hear it from "The Master."

As we arrived, there was Fred, standing erect and confident in front of an assortment of parents and kids, ready to dispense his own distinctive brand of baseball wisdom. At one point in his presentation, he encouraged the kids to "come home after school, get out a baseball, and throw it against the garage or a nearby wall;" at which point he launched into that repetitive patter of his, accompanied by slashing hand gestures and arm motions, all designed to drive home his main idea...that practice, practice, practice, and more practice is the key to achievement: "just throw the ball, throw the ball, throw the ball, throw the ball..."

Hearing this, my mind involuntarily flashed back 30 years to my own days as one of Fred Heinlen's high school ball players. I could and can still hear the staccato-like cadences, the rapid succession of one-syllable words, coming at you over and over again, each word given great emphasis and building, so often (or so it seemed), to a crescendo of rebuke: "Klein, can't you get the ball over the plate?" And I remembered then, and still remember now, what I desperately wanted to say to him at those moments, but didn't have the courage to: "Mr. Heinlen, believe me, I'm trying."

110

Speaking of trying but with too little success...I remember, during so many a ball game, watching Mr. Heinlen trudging out to the pitcher's mound, his face all full of desperation and disappointment, relieving me of the baseball while repeating, "Klein, why can't you just get the ball over the plate?" And I remember walking to the bench, passing my replacements, and then waiting for Mr. Heinlen (he was "Fred" only behind his back) to come and sit next to me and to try once again to get me to see how elementary a thing getting the ball over the plate really is.

Indelible image: Fred Heinlen running around the high school track, day after day, by himself...his hair cut short, his body lean and youthful, his eyes focused and purposeful. Why is it that so many of us, when we think of Fred, see him in our mind's eye running endlessly around that track, eternally young and vigorous and thinking only about physical fitness and the glorious rush that such fitness brings to those who have it and who are able to use it?

For all the gruffness of his demeanor, Fred Heinlen remains one of the formative influences of my life. I think it was the combination of his passion for the game of baseball, his obvious mastery of all aspects of the sport, his intensity and focus, his love of victory, his dedication to us, his ball players, and his desire to see his charges mature and excel and feel the exhilaration of achievement. And these passions and ideals, imparted to us by his actions as well as his words, remain with so many of us who were privileged to have him as teacher and coach and mentor.

Robert Lebby
Shaker Heights High School - Class of 1969
BA - Duke University
MS - George Williams College
Owner/Director, North Star Camp for Boys, Hayward, Wisconsin
Partner, "TNT, The Network Team"

Whenever I watch a baseball game I think about Fred. He was such a good coach! He taught us not only the fundamentals of baseball but made the subtle beauties of the game come alive. Coach loved baseball and those that spent time with him couldn't help but be touched by the game.

As a coach he implored us to do our best and to try our hardest at all times. I can still remember his halftime football speech, when he told us that we would always remember how hard we played in our last game; that we would look back and either be proud or disappointed in our effort; that once the game was over there was nothing we could do to bring it back or no way to do it over again. What I didn't realize at the time was that Coach Heinlen used sports as a metaphor for life. He wasn't just coaching us in baseball or football, but coaching us in life.

What really blew me away was the personalized letter he sent me last year, 32 years after my high school graduation. He was just letting me know that I was remembered and then he gave me some examples of what he remembered about me in high school. He made me proud, he made me cry and he helped me to realize that adults can continue to have an impact on "their" kids long after the kids become adults. Coach Heinlen is still coaching me, 32 years after my last game with him. WOW!!!

Bill Needle
Cleveland Heights High School - Class of 1965

1971-1979 Baseball and Basketball Coach, Shaw High School, Cleveland, Ohio
1980-Director of Communications, Cleveland Cavaliers
1991-Present, National and local Broadcaster, Fox Sports Net

Fred made coaching look simple - not easy, but simple. His baseball teams were fundamentally impeccable. It seems as though they never made a mental mistake. They might lose - my teams even had a modest winning streak against them - but an opponent had to defeat Fred's teams because they never beat themselves.

He didn't over-coach. I'll always remember him telling his teams, "Get one twice," in double play situations, or "Let's just win the inning," to keep them focused on the task at hand.

Certainly, he had good players. But he always seemed to get the most out of the average kid - the kid who didn't end up with a pro contract or in a Division I program. As I remember, those were the kids who always seemed to beat us - the kids who always seemed to know what to do, no matter the situation. Fred deserves the credit for that.

I remember a college professor saying, "There is an art that conceals art." Perhaps that phrase best sums up Fred Heinlen's coaching. He never looked like he was coaching. In the meantime, while looking like he wasn't coaching, his teams managed to win league, sectional, regional, district and State championships.

It was an honor to coach against him - and the greatest victories of my coaching career came whenever my team beat his. I remember those victories almost pitch-by-pitch - as if they were yesterday, instead of a quarter-century ago.

He is legendary. His legacy will endure forever.

113

Bob Rawson
Shaker Heights High School, Class of 1962
  BA - Princeton University
  MA - Rhodes Scholar, Oxford University
  JD - Harvard University
  Partner in Charge & Lawyer, Jones Day, Cleveland, Ohio
  President, Board of Trustees, Princeton University

My first impressions of Fred were formed as a callow sophomore. He was disciplined, demanding but eminently fair, knowledgeable and willing to reward effort, tenacity and devotion to team principles even in a youngster whose talents were somewhat limited. He is the same man today he was then - Fred is nothing if not constant.

I played basketball for Fred with a group of determined, intelligent athletes. But we were small and slow and always the underdog. Fred could not make us taller, and he could not make us any faster. But he made us much smarter by teaching us a team concept that gave us a chance to win against anybody. In fact, we beat three of the top ten teams in the city in consecutive games.

But baseball was, and is, Fred's game. It was in the context of baseball that he contributed the most to this one young athlete. When our star third baseman suffered a serious injury, Fred installed me in the position as a still callow sophomore starting out over his head. When I struggled, Fred said: "Never mind, you're our third baseman!" Because he believed in me, I subsequently found my confidence and my game. No coach, no mentor, no friend (and Fred has been all three) can do more for a young boy than that.

For three school years, I spent at least two hours per day, five or sometimes six, days per week, and plenty of time each summer, under Fred's tutelage. I experienced more than a few Fred-managed batting practices, passing drills, weight lifting, base running, free throws, endless sprints, etc. And I am much the better for that time spent learning that anything worth doing is worth doing right; that the fundamentals matter; and the strong may take from the weak - but the smart will take from the strong.

Thanks Fred!

John Pearson
Shaker Heights High School - Class of 1966
BA - Marietta College
Master of Divinity - Andover Newton Theological School
President & Chief Executive Officer, BIG Brothers of Massachusetts Bay

My senior year in high school (the year following the State baseball championship), we had a practice and Fred pulled me aside and said: "You're the only pitcher I have. The other thing you have to know is that I've learned something about you; my style of coaching is not best for you. I'm used to hot shot high school athletes who need to be taken down a peg because they think they are God's gift to things, but really they need to work harder. You are the most self critical athlete that I've coached. So when I get on you, I know that I'm just doing the wrong thing. You have my permission if I'm every saying: "now Judas Priest Pearson, throw the ball over the plate!" to stop the game, call time-out, call me out to the mound and just say, "Who are you going to put in Fred? I will turn around, I will sit down on the bench and I will shut up because I'm going to go with you."

Fred's comments summarize his character. He taught me, through his own action, to recognize your own strengths and to be able to adjust when the situation calls for it, a valuable lesson I never forgot.

Jessie Roberson
Shaker Heights High School - Class of 1972
AB - Princeton University
JD - University of Michigan
MBA - University of Toronto
Associate Professor, Business Law - Ohio University

My dad died eight days before my ninth birthday and my family moved to Shaker Heights shortly thereafter. A few years later, I met Fred Heinlen while hanging around the local high school's backstop. I was big for my age and, by seventh grade, Coach let me practice with his high school team. For the next decade, he was the most important male figure in my life. Truth be told, my secret hope was to someday succeed him as baseball coach at Shaker High. My fondest memories of adolescence relate in one way or another to lessons learned hanging around that baseball diamond.

He taught me all manner of things: the niceties of catcher footwork; variations on slider grips; how to tie a proper bowtie. At some point in time, he was my coach in football, basketball and baseball. My favorite, and his, was baseball. Most of us came to share his dream, winning the State baseball championship and spending the night before the championship game in the Neil House Hotel in downtown Columbus.

He taught me everything I know about competition. We always played to win, but what mattered most was HOW you competed. You couldn't control what the other guy did. You couldn't control who would prevail. You could control what you put into every practice, every game, every day. You could be sure you had done all you could, physically and mentally, to give yourself the optimal opportunity to win. If you did that, most of the time, you would win. And if you lost, it was because the other guy was better, not because you did something to screw it up.

116

On rainy days, we sometimes moved practice indoors. Often part of those practices was spent doing chalk talks of game situations and talking about life. Coach Heinlen taught us the importance of trying to prepare ourselves to be successful. He would buttress these life-lessons with readings, everything from Ted Williams's, *The Science of Hitting* to Og Mandino's, *The Greatest Salesman on Earth.*

To a more or less normal group of teen-aged boys, his myriad approaches met with varying levels of acceptance. I will never forget one spring afternoon when Coach, in the middle of diagraming proper execution of cut-off plays, lapsed into a discourse on the importance of relishing the handful of truly "big events" one experiences in life. In response to a look of obvious dismay from one of my teammates, Heinlen stopped and said, "I'll bet some of you wonder why I take time to talk to you about stuff like this. Years from now, if all you've gotten from all these hours you spend with me is having chased a little ball around a field, this time is wasted."

To my mind, that sums up what coaching is supposed to be about. Athletics can teach lessons that are hard to learn anyplace else. Schools and parents entrust their kids to grown-ups who are supposed to help those children become better adults. Too many coaches get caught up in the moment and lose that point. Coach Heinlen never did. He is a critical part of the best parts of what I have done with my life. I will always love him for that.

George Roth
Shaker Heights High School - Class of 1961

BA - Tulane University
President, George Roth, Inc., Real Estate Consulting, Cleveland, Ohio

Fred Heinlen's knowledge of baseball far surpasses that of many major league baseball players. My opinion was confirmed when I attended a baseball fantasy camp. "Judas Priest!" Many of those major leaguers "coaches" did not even know how to defend the play where t
he runner on first base purposely got picked off while the runner on third scored without even a play!

The intricacies of baseball that Coach Heinlen taught us at an early age have given many of us countless hours of pleasure while watching baseball games for years. The true beauty of the game can be appreciated by those who had the benefit of Fred Heinlen's coaching.

Van Seasholes
Shaker Heights High School - Class of 1951

BA - Amherst College
MA - Harvard University
Retired Principal, Newton South High School, Newton Centre, Massachusetts

I first saw Fred in action in late August 1946. It was sometime after the traditional August 20th starting day for football practice, so Fred must have been 31. He was the new head basketball, baseball and assistant football coach at Shaker Heights High School. I was a 13 year old eighth grader who was looking forward to playing all three sports. Fred's enthusiasm, knowledge, and skill were evident that day as they still are 56 years later.

Fred was a neighbor of ours on Chadbourne Road and I have always enjoyed visiting with him on my return trips to Cleveland. Although he spent endless hours in coaching year around, his family - his wife, Lois, and children, Doug, Rodd, and Jan - was always his first priority. Their mutual support, respect, and love were always clear.

Fred has always kept himself in great shape. He was an early advocate of running and thoughtful eating habits. It shows today, for he is a fit, healthy, vigorous 86 years young.

Dennis Goodman
Shaker Heights High School - Class of 1956
AB - Dartmouth College
MA - John Hopkins University
Retired Foreign Service Operator, US Department of State

During my two years on varsity basketball, we were at best a .500 team. Our tallest guys were Kahn and Tamcsin, at about 6'2". I played center at 5'11" so you can guess that we didn't run over anyone. But we were always better coached than the opposition, and that, above anything else, is what I want to say about Fred. We all laughed at the "Judas Priest" and "Paaathetic" comments he regularly made. Today when we get together, we still do. W all know that we never played another basketball team that was as well schooled as we were. The one thing he couldn't coach us to do was to grow another six inches.

Angelo Valenti
Shaker Heights High School - Class of 1966
BA - Case Western Reserve University
MA & Ph.D - University of Georgia
Consulting Psychologist & Owner, The Company Psychologist

With the exception of my grandfather and Uncle Sam, Coach Heinlen had more influence on my life than any other man. Unfortunately, I did not realize all that he was teaching me until many years after I had left Shaker.

The thing that stands out about Coach was his unwavering sense of integrity. He had high standards, he had definite ideas about the right way to do things, and he did not compromise those principles in the heat of the moment. His moral compass was always pointed at true north. I am sure that some people found him to be inflexible, but to me he was like a lighthouse. I didn't always like it, but I knew where I stood.

He benched me a couple of times, and I deserved it both times. The first episode occurred the week after we had played Lakewood in JV football. We played a terrible game and got killed. After our next practice, Coach made us run laps. I ran them as slowly as I could without walking, and when I finished Coach asked me why I ran so slowly. I replied: "If I wanted to run laps, I would have gone out for the track team." Coach looked me in the eye and said, "I know that is your way of telling me to go to hell, but you are a leader on this team and I expect more from you. You can watch the next game from the stands." The next game was against Cleveland Heights, our biggest rivals, and we didn't really have a second string quarterback. I watched us get beat and never forgot how it felt to let my teammates down.

The second time he benched me was for not sliding into home. This was just laziness on my part, but I made sure I always slid and gave each play 100% after that.

The thing I remember most about Coach's coaching philosophy was his emphasis on fundamentals. To this day, I believe I know more about baseball than 99.9% of the people in the world, and I learned it from him. When we played "situation," we did it with a vengeance, but when those situations came up in games, everyone knew exactly what to do. I believe we hit more cutoff men, backed up more bases, ran down more runners properly, and bunted more effectively than any high school team I ever saw. I'll stack up our championship team against any high school team of that era.

I also remember what Coach said about hitting. He told me that hitting a baseball was the single hardest athletic act there was. I still believe that to be true. He said that he could teach almost anyone to hit a ball, but he couldn't teach him to be a hitter. I remember the three C's of hitting: Courage, Confidence and Concentration. He used to tell me that I was the only good hitter he ever had that had so much Confidence and Concentration, that I could get by with a lack of Courage. It took me a long time to learn courage, but I'm getting there. Those three C's work pretty well outside of the batter's box as well.

Thanks for giving me a chance to reflect on a truly great man.

*Excerpts from **News Herald** sports page,
Monday, August 14, 2000: To Know Heinlen Is Blessing
Enough*

He often types letters to folks he thinks are deserving of a
kind word and always his closing line is "Blessings a-plenty."
Among my blessings a-plenty is to know Fred Heinlen.
Today, Fred will be 85 years young and he's more deserving
of accolades and publicity - which he never seeks - than most
of the athletes this column has spotlighted.

Fred is and has been a man for all sports, a teacher, a coach,
an official. Those who have played the games in this state
have been touched by his hand, although many may not have
realized it until today.

For years, Fred ran baseball clinics for the Indians, going all
over Ohio's highways and byways to work with coaches and
the kids, passing along his knowledge and his philosophy.
The latter, I'm proud to say, also is mine: Teach the kids the
fundamentals and let them play the game. Don't be carping
and criticizing. Sit back and let them have the fun of playing.
When the Indians dropped the clinics from their budget, Fred
continued them to this day, no charge. Just call him. He'll be
there.

It was Fred who caused some major changes in the way
baseball is introduced to youngsters. While coaching Shaker
Heights High School to two State titles, he also handled the
summer baseball program for the city. He saw kids shaking
in the batter's box as the wild kids on the mound threw

122

everywhere but over the plate. He saw the other kids standing around at their positions because the hitters weren't hitting. So he decided the kids should start out playing slow pitch and adults should be doing the pitching, throwing the ball nice and easy over the plate. Also they would play T-ball, so all the position players got into the game. When ready, they would advance to live pitching, kids to kids, and the real game. The Heinlen plan caught on in many communities because it worked.

Bob Rice, a fellow teacher at Shaker says, "Fred always marched to his own drum. He always dared to be different." Beating that drum is a thoughtful, compassionate heart. If someone he knows is in the hospital, Fred will make a quick visit, say an encouraging word, drop off an appropriate item and just as quickly disappear. He wants no thanks.

Last week, after my induction into the writers' wing of the Baseball Hall of Fame, my bride received a letter from Fred. It read: "How strange that on the platform (in Cooperstown) those guys aren't standing next to their brides, the force behind their accomplishments, the encouragement, understanding, without which all of them would be standing at the bottom of the mountain, rather than on top. Take a bow, Mrs. Hal. And now that the festivities are over tell him to get out and mow the lawn...Blessings a-plenty."

Fred was so right. Without our brides, we'd be nothing. Same with him. He and Lois have been married 58 years. It takes an understanding wife to allow a Fred Heinlen to march to his own drum.

His grandson Carson now plays baseball for Shaker and his coach, Buddy Longo, once played for Shaker. Longo's coach: Fred Heinlen. At the Shaker ball field is a first-class electric scoreboard. A large rock under it, to which is attached a metal plaque, reveals the scoreboard is a gift from "The friends of Fred Heinlen and the Class of 1961. Fred told Carson, "I want you to pat that rock when you run past it onto the field." Carson did, and a teammate said, "What are you patting that rock for? He's just an old guy who's not around anymore." Replied Carson: "That guy is my granddad and he's very much around."

Thank heaven. Happy 85th today, Fred. And blessings a-plenty.

THE END